Rage
and
Celebration

Rage
and
Celebration

*Essays on
Contemporary Afro-American
Writing*

by
Sigmund Ro

HUMANITIES PRESS: New Jersey

SOLUM FORLAG A.S.: Oslo

First published in 1984 in Norway by SOLUM FORLAG A.S and in the United States of America by HUMANITIES PRESS INC., Atlantic Highlands, NJ 07716.

© Copyright 1984 by Solum Forlag A.S.
Cover design: Jan Pahle

Financially supported by Norges almenvitenskapelige forsknings-råd (The Norwegian Research Council for Science and the Humanities).

ISBN 0-391-03094-9 (Humanities)
ISBN 82-560-0315-4 (Solum)

Printed in Norway by
S. Hammerstad Boktrykkeri, Oslo.

For Anne Karin

Contents

Preface

For a Scandinavian to venture into the field of black American studies may seem a hazardous undertaking. In addition to the often exasperating practical problem of access to source materials, there are the subtler difficulties of penetrating beyond the surface of statistics and sociological data to a deeper grasp of a minority culture as distinctive as that of Afro-America. Such a grasp must be the prerequisite of any effort to study black literary expression, and the transatlantic outsider can only hope to achieve at least a basic familiarity with the cultural complexities behind the written literature.

The bulk of these reflections on contemporary writing by black Americans — creative and critical — were produced in 1978 and 1979. The first essay attempts to capture the mood of the transition period from the first to the second postwar decade through a close reading of two stories by James Baldwin and William Melvin Kelley (originally published in *American Studies in Scandinavia,* 1975: 17-47.) The others focus on the 1960s in terms of what is seen as a distinctive and major thematic design of the decade: rage and celebration. I have wished to avoid any use of this pattern as a straightjacket, applying it instead as a lens through which the literary innovations of the period come into focus in terms of how they creatively reenact past materials. In the second essay, an attempt is made to study the transformation of the classic duality of rage and celebration under the impact of the Third World revolution. The last two are more limited studies of how the same dual theme is seen operating in two representative autobiographical narratives and in the fiction of John A. Williams, whose development in the 1960s offers a paradigm of the major tensions and currents of the decade.

I wish to thank the Norwegian Research Council for Science and the Humanities and the University of Trondheim for financial assistance and a leave of absence that enabled me to finish the writing. Thanks are also due to John A. Williams, who received me so hospitably when I visited New York in November of 1978. Lastly, I owe a debt to students and colleagues with whom I have engaged in discussion of the works, the writers, and the issues included. Their suggestions have been most helpful. Remaining errors are — as Samuel Johnson said — the result of «ignorance . . . sheer ignorance.»

The Black Musician as Literary Hero: Baldwin's «Sonny's Blues» and Kelley's «Cry for Me»

This essay presents two case studies of the intellectual and ideological sources of the black hero in Afro-American fiction. The two stories by James Baldwin and William Melvin Kelley have been selected because they are representative of their times and provide convenient mirrors of intellectual and ideological continuities and discontinuities in black American writing in the postwar era.

Art and culture intersect. To look at fictional heroes is at the same time to be looking at refracted images of cultural realities beyond the internal verbal structures of the literary artifact. In the words of Edmund Fuller, «every man's novel may not have a *thesis,* but it must have a *premise* — whether declared or tacit, whether conscious or unconscious.» [1] That premise, without which no work of literature can be coherent or even intelligible, must ultimately be located in the extraliterary and extralinguistic reality of the writer's culture. Character is perhaps the formal component most immediately dependent on such nonliterary premises.

Black fiction in the postwar period illustrates this interdependence between society and art with particular clarity. In the first decade, the spirit of the black intellectual community was characterized by integrationist views and a wish to join the mainstream of American literary life. This tendency was exemplified by the use of white characters, milieus, and authorial postures in Ann Petry's and Willard Motley's fiction, and further buttressed by an emerging black critical establishment in the 1940s and 1950s, trained in Northern graduate schools and rigorously applying the literary standards of white critics.

Saunders Redding, Nick Aaron Ford, Nathan Scott, and Hugh Gloster were all agreed in urging black artists to emancipate themselves from «the fetters of racial chauvinism»[2] and to deal with universal human experience.

In retrospect, it is not hard to discern the broader cultural context of this trend in black literary expression and criticism. In the
overall effort of the black minority to achieve a position of equality in society, the strategy was understandably to emphasize the
common humanity of black and white at the expense of the ethno-
centricity of the interwar period. The same tendency prevailed in
the Jewish-American community. In literary terms, this meant insistence on the writer's freedom to deal with his material in a non-
racialist and universal spirit. Specifically, it meant literary characters created or interpreted in terms of archetypes or generalized
human identity quests. In accordance with this mood, John
Grimes of *Go Tell It on the Mountain* and Ellison's unnamed hero
as well as Bellow's and Malamud's Jews were read as symbols of
Youth, the Artist, or the human condition.

In this light, Baldwin's bestknown short story, «Sonny's Blues»
(1957),[3] merits reconsideration in terms of the modern Euro-
American intellectual stance underlying it that appears to have
escaped critical notice.

Reflected in Baldwin's portrait of a black blues artist is, for all his
discovery of racial community noted by commentators, the whole
integration ethos of the first postwar decade, stated in the familiar
existentialist categories of the Left Bank coteries in which Baldwin
moved between 1948 and 1958. Though not actively seeking admission to the white world, Sonny is conceived in the image of
Kierkegaard-Sartre-Camus and provided with an authentic black
exterior. Behind Sonny there looms the nonracial esthetic of the
Baldwin who proclaimed in 1955 that he merely wanted to be «an
honest man and a good writer.»[4]

With the radicalization of the civil rights movement, the new
militant nationalism, and the impact of African liberation, the
literary situation for the black writer changed, spelling the end of
the esthetic upon which Baldwin's Sonny was predicted. *Negritude*
or *soul* gradually became a focal point of black cultural activity,
involving separatist notions of artistic creation and the role of the
artist.

The dimension of *Negritude* that has informed so much recent
black writing is less the political implications of Pan-Africanism
than the highly effective mystique of blackness as a special moral
and spiritual sensibility that has evolved out of the writings of such

theoreticians as Aimé Césaire, Alioune Diop, and Léopold Senghor.[5] Here *Negritude* is thought of as a distinct ethos; that is, a body of traits, habits, and values crystallized into a peculiar lifestyle and producing a psychology common not only to black Africans, but to blacks living in the American diaspora as well. It involves a sense of self and community that derives from an exclusive group identity forged by a unique historical experience or even, as intimated by Senghor, having its origin in biological-genetic facts. It is a condition as well as a fate, preceding and transcending the vicissitudes of economics, politics, and history. Thus, at the 1956 Conference of Negro African Writers and Artists in Paris, Senghor could appeal to American blacks to reinterpret their literature in terms of their common heritage of *Negritude,* taking himself the first step by discussing Richard Wright's poetry and *Black Boy* as African works.

In America, the corresponding concept of *soul,* if not the word itself, existed well before the historical *Negritude* movement. Although not interchangeable concepts, they share a vision of a «Soul Force,»[6] a unique source of moral and spiritual energy, peculiar to blacks everywhere. The real boost of the *soul* ethos and its political and literary application, however, occurred with the coinciding emergence of the latest phase of the civil rights movement in the United States and the African liberation from European colonialism in the late 1950s. The impact of *soul* was soon felt in black writing, especially as LeRoi Jones's seminal influence made itself felt after 1964, and led, in its extreme form, to a deemphasizing of the mimetic principle of the Western conception of art and its traditional distinction between «art» and «life», stressing instead the oral, utilitarian, and communal nature of African art as an ideal for black Americans to emulate.

Of the writers responding to the new currents, William Melvin Kelley has established himself as a major figure. As the decade of the 1960s unfolded, he found himself carried farther and farther away from the assimilationist position from which he started out. Trained at the exclusive Fieldstone School in New York before admission to Harvard and teaching posts at the New School for Social Research and Bard College, he started out in the familiar style of the privileged «token Negro» bent on seeking acceptance and success in white America. At first, his artistic credo gave no cause

for alarm. His self-confessed intention, as stated in the preface to
Dancers on the Shore,[7] was reassuringly within the accepted
pattern of depicting human reality in universal terms, conceiving
of himself as a detached artist with no obligations to provide social
and political answers.

Even as he was stating his credo, however, Kelley was troubled
by its inadequacies. Not unlike LeRoi Jones, whose startingpoint
had been similar to his own, he found himself moving closer to a
militant and racial esthetic under the impact of social and ideological developments in the black community. His public break with
white American came in 1967, two years after Jones's defection
from the New York literary establishment whose favorite talent he
had become.

The beginnings of Kelley's new *ars poetica,* derived from *soul*
and committing him to the creation of a racial art addressed to
black audiences, can be traced back even to his earliest work. The
work that most clearly pinpoints this transition process is perhaps
the story entitled «Cry for Me» (1962)[8] which, in spite of the preface to *Dancers on the Shore,* where it was first published, be-
speaks a growing restlessness with previous esthetic assumptions
and a sympathetic response to the *soul* ethos that he now appears
to have embraced with few qualifications. Appropriately placed at
the end of the volume, this story foreshadows ideas to be further
developed and reinforced in his later fiction while at the same time
typifying the changing character of black literary expression in the
past decade. Together, Baldwin's and Kelley's two stories provide
interesting case studies of what happens to fiction when it is subjected to the pressures of ideological change.

1.

The two stories lend themselves particularly well to a comparative
analysis of the black literary hero because the external formal
frameworks are so similar. The geographical settings overlap almost completely. Except for short excursions into the Bronx
neighborhood of Carlyle's family, both stories move within a
world circumscribed, physically as well as symbolically, by

Harlem and Greenwich Village. In both, Village cabarets play central roles as scenes of epiphanic illuminations in the lives of the two narrators. To each story the urban setting is indispensible either as the source of the peculiar strains and frustrations of the characters or as a foil to the unadulterated preurban black «soul».
The characters operate within the same structural pattern. In each case, the story hinges on the opposition of two characters, related by blood, but opposed in every other respect. One is a bourgeois Negro and the narrator of the story, the other is a «soul» character with no desire to join the middle-class Establishment to which his relative belongs or to which he aspires. Sonny's brother is already firmly ensconced in the black bourgeoisie, while Carlyle appears to be bent on making it in the white world into which his family has moved since its beginnings in Harlem. In both cases, the development of the characters lends itself to description in terms of the «initiation» pattern. Carlyle and Sonny's brother both grow from either a state of ignorance or guilty innocence to higher levels of consciousness through contact with their relatives. This pattern is also the principle governing the two plots. In either case, a narrator whose presumed superiority makes him adopt the role of teacher and authority, receives a relative who is seen as ignorant, innocent, or immature. Ironically, both plots proceed to overturn this relationship by reversing their relative positions. By the end of the stories, the visitors have become the teachers and authorities by virtue of their charisma and insight while the narrators have been relegated to the position of humble apprentices and recipients of their mentors' messages. Thus the narrative structures are made to serve the educational process in the two characters initiated into the mysteries communicated by the black heroes whose medium of expression is, in both cases, music. Finally, the realism of the two stories is modified by the same set of symbols and images. Sonny and Uncle Wallace both become high priests and their concerts ceremonial occasions reenacting semireligious dramas of sacrifice and redemption.

This formal resemblance makes the differences in the larger implications of the two musician-heroes stand out all the more clearly. It would seem, however, from the criticism elicited by «Sonny's Blues», that this aspect has not been given the attention it deserves. Commentators appear unanimous in their emphasis on

the racial element as it appears in the hero's individual identity
quest within the boundaries of black culture.

Both Marcus Klein and Shirley Anne Williams agree that the
thrust of Sonny's message is the expression of his black identity.
He is, in Klein's words, «full of unspecified Negroness», his problem is the «burden of his racial identity» to be expressed through
his music. Ultimately, the story undertakes to reveal «the Negro
motives that may issue in the blues».[9] Shirley Williams is willing to
see Sonny as the typical alienated artist of so much twentieth-century literature, but she insists that his main «referent is Black lives,
Black experiences and Black deaths.» His estrangement is primarily an estrangement from his «ancestral past».[10] The cure can only
be effected through a restoration of the relationship between his
personal history and that of his racial group. This delicate, but
healing balance between private and group selves Sonny is finally
able to achieve in his solo performance within the context of
Creole's jazz band. On the other hand, Edward Margolies sees
Sonny's music as a means of self-expression reflecting Baldwin's
Christian-Protestant heritage. Even so, however, he sees Sonny's
outbursts of «the grief and terror that rage within his soul» as
patterned on the testimony of the redeemed saint in the presence of
witnesses, presumably to be equated with the audience, thus ultimately relating the story to the black religious tradition of the store-
front church as the context of the protagonist's identity quest.[11]

It cannot of course be denied that Sonny's art is conditioned by
racial factors. His despair is the despair of the sensitive black
ghetto youngster feeling the stifling effect of his environment. His
need to escape is easily attributable to fear of victimization by the
same forces that turn his brother's students into drug addicts or
naturally sensuous women into the frenziedly pious church sisters
testifying in the street. The music has a direct therapeutic function,
permitting him to contain his pentup frustration and even enabling
him to temporarily transcend his circumstances. Sonny needs his
music to master his potentially self-destructive anger at being
trapped in a black slum. He must play in order not to smash some-
body's skull; his music is a form of mental hygiene. In this respect,
the psychology involved is essentially the same as that of other
musician- or artist-heroes in Baldwin's work or in Clay Williams's
Dutchman.

As Sonny realizes the deeper implications of what he is playing, his music acquires the significance it has in *Go Tell It on the Mountain* and in Baldwin's essays: that of putting himself and his audience in touch with their common ancestral past. In the final scene, it evokes in his brother's mind the reality of family, forefathers, and community in black life. Memories are stirred of childhood scenes of Sunday afternoon reunions of relatives and «church folks» huddled together against the darkness of the outside world. In an attempt to impress upon him the necessity of protecting Sonny, their mother tells him of the murder of his uncle by white men and the traumatic effect of this experience on her husband. At the piano, Sonny becomes a high priest invoking the collective and accumulated experience of «that long line, of which we know only Mama and Daddy» — one of the central images in the first novel — and mediating with the authority of a shaman between the living and the dead members of the tribe. Throughout this ever-expanding perspective from present into past, from personal experience into family history and the history of «that long line», this telescoped racial history, captured and reenacted by Baldwin's musician-hero, is evoked literarily in the story in images of light and darkness. There is a consistent — and ironic — association of light with black community feeling and togetherness and of darkness with a racist and oppressive white world. Thus Sonny's music has an unmistakable racial core. It functions as a means of escape from the ghetto and as a psychological buffer to his bruised black ego by enabling him to identify with and draw strength from the past and the present group experience of his race.

This concern with his racial heritage is a prominent feature in Baldwin's other early work as well. Originally intending to escape the burden of race through a self-imposed exile, he gradually discovered the futility of such an endeavor. Cast in the form of the personal myth writers often create of their artistic coming of age, his account in «Stranger in the Village»[12] tells the story of how he immured himself in a Swiss village armed only with a typewriter and Bessie Smith records in order to put himself through the painful process of overcoming his feelings of shame and self-hatred through unconditional self-acceptance. Out of this experience was born his first novel. The problem of self-acceptance continued to haunt him, however, until he returned to make peace with his native land and go South in search of his ancestral roots in the late 1950s. Written in 1956—57, «Sonny's Blues» can be directly related to the author's concern, during the first postwar decade, with coming to terms with the fact and meaning of being black in a racist white world that imposes upon its racial minorities its own notions of superiority and inferiority. The resulting syndromes of self-destructive flight into «white» values and behavior patterns and the opposite impulse of revolt generated by this imposition are demonstrated by the narrator and Sonny respectively. In fact, one might view this antithetical grouping of the two main characters as a reflection of the latent tension in Baldwin's own imagination between his ambivalently alternating identifications with the black masses and the world of the black and white middle-class in a way that is strongly reminiscent of Langston Hughes's self-confessed projection of similar conflicting impulses in himself into the folk character Jesse B. Simple and the genteel, intellectual narrator in his wartime sketches in the *Chicago Defender*.

In Baldwin's story this tension is resolved in favor of Sonny's identification with his racial past and his brother's «conversion» to a similar position, symbolized by the ritual of sharing a sacramental drink in the final scene. This racial self-acceptance is, however, a more complex matter than has hitherto been recognized. While certainly genuine and valid in racial terms, the identity achieved ultimately transcends race to become a statement on the human condition in the modern world in a universal sense. Furthermore, it can be demonstrated in considerable detail that the story's universalizing formula derives from the concepts and, occasionally, the explicit vocabulary, of contemporary existentialist thought.

As already pointed out, Baldwin's story in this respect parallels the familiar pattern in postwar literature and criticism of employing racial heroes as archetypes of the modern human predicament. Characteristically, Jean-Paul Sartre's interest in Richard Wright's work is based on the supposed susceptibility of the alienated outsider-victim to interpretation in general existentialist terms. Black critic Esther Merle Jackson's essay, «The American Negro and the Image of the Absurd,» rests on the assumption that there is an essential likeness between Bigger Thomas, Ellison's invisible man, and Faulkner's Joe Christmas on the one hand, and, on the other hand, the heroes of Dostoevsky, Proust, Gide, Malraux, Mann, and Sartre.[13] Indeed, in the case of *Native Son* and *The Outsider,* it has become almost a critical commonplace to regard their black protagonists as symbols of suffering, alienated, rebelling mankind.In the same critical tradition, the theologian-critic Nathan A. Scott has pointed to the kinship of Wright's writings with what he calls «a main tradition in the spiritual history of the modern world.»[14] Scott's specific reference is to the French-inspired existentialist mode of thought, notably in Camus's version, and the grounds for the alleged sameness of the black and the existentialist experience is the analogy of the Negro's historical familiarity with anxiety, violence, rejection, nihilism, and revolt with similar phenomena in Europe as a result of the ravages of global war and totalitarian politics. The reality of the concentration camp — whether in Germany or in Mississippi — is the common ground on which the black American and the modern European meet. Scott's analogy should be treated with caution, but its expressive power is not lightly dismissed.

Indeed, the basis for such a parallelism between the black experience and the condition of modern man was prepared by Wright himself in his threefold conception of Bigger as simultaneously a «bad nigger», proletarian class hero, and a symbol of uprooted modern man in an industrial and technological civilization.[15] This was further emphasized and elaborated in *White Man, Listen!* (1957), where he reminded his European audience that the Negro, brutally uprooted from his tribal origins in Africa and transplanted to a Western world already in the throes of the industrial revolution, epitomizes the fate of the Westerners themselves in the modern world:

> So, in historical outline, the lives of American Negroes closely resemble your own. . . . The history of the Negro in America is the history of America written in vivid and bloody terms; it is the history of Western Man writ small. It is the history of man who tried to adjust themselves to a world whose laws, customs, and instruments of force were leveled against them. The Negro is America's metaphor.[16]

In his own fiction, Wright dramatized this universal perspective
not only in the character of Bigger Thomas, but even more explicitly in Fred Daniels in «The Man Who Lived Underground»
(1944) and in Cross Damon.

The same tendency to see the Negro in universal and symbolic
terms is present in Baldwin's work in the 1950s, prompted by the
same desire after the war to play down racial differences in favor
of a global vision of mankind and environmental explanations of
racial characteristics. After his disappointing encounter with black
Africans in Paris, he discovered the close resemblance of his own
experience with that of white Americans: «In white Americans
(the American Negro) finds reflected — repeated, as it were, in a
higher key — his tensions, his terror, his tenderness.»[17] The
experience is the same as Wright's, except that, interestingly, for
Baldwin it seems to be the other way round: It is the white man's
condition that epitomizes his own.

Thus Baldwin and his musician-hero can be seen as placed
squarely within the mainstream of both black and white racial
thought in the first postwar decade. Intellectually, they are akin to
the ontology and idiom constituting the framework of black
writing before the racial revolution of the 1960s, reflecting the
prevailing ideology of a black intelligentsia striving to deemphasize
the stigma of race through integration and universalizing
formulas. Through the twist he gives to Wright's metaphor, Baldwin reveals the ideological perspective of his first postwar position.
Somewhat unkindly put, the implicit strategy is to plead for the
Negro's equal worth by stressing that the same «tensions,»
«terror,» and «tenderness» that move the white man also move
him. The closeness of this argument to the white liberal position is
neatly revealed by comparing it to the premise of Kenneth
Stampp's study of slavery from 1956: «innately Negroes *are,* after
all, only white men with black skins, nothing more, nothing
less.»[18] It is within this larger context that Sonny yields up
meanings beyond his narrowly racial significance that critics so far
have tended to stress. In the effort to make him a modern man
fully as human as his white brother, Baldwin turned to the concepts and vocabulary of existentialism flowing into Europe and
America from the Paris in which he was living. On this background, Sonny acquires a definable «intellectual physiognomy»[19]

and his ideological implications can be more clearly perceived. It is significant that the straining toward integrated and universalizing statements on man's existential condition has a special urgency in the case of black heroes. In the 1950s, it was imperative to assert the universal humanity of the racial hero in order to overcome the tragic legacy of racism in Western culture.

This is not to say that Sonny is an intellectual or a simple embodiment of clear-cut ideological aims. As George Lukacs points out, a literary character does not have to operate consciously on a high level of abstraction and verbal articulateness in order to have an intellectual physiognomy. Nor is there any need for authorial analysis and comment. Intellectual assumptions and attitudes are, and indeed should be, embedded in the whole range of responses to the pressures to which he is subjected. In Baldwin's story, instead of conceptualizing and articulating his hard-won insight verbally to his brother, Sonny prefers to expose him directly to its musical expression. Similarly, his brother's «conversion» to Sonny's message is not presented in terms of intellectual discovery, but as a direct revelation and a ritualized initiation suggested by his symbolic nonverbal gesture of buying a sacramental «Scotch and milk» for Sonny as a token of their communal sharing of a new wisdom. Sonny's intellectual profile and ideological significance emerge from the totality of his story, not from self-conscious philosophical contemplation or crude propaganda statements.

The existentialist concept most immediatey visible in Baldwin's story is the Sartrean distinction between authentic and inauthentic living. Central to Sartre's distinction is the idea of self-delusion. Having defined man's situation as «one of free choice, without excuse and without help,» he argues that «any man who takes refuge behind the excuse of passion, or by inventing some deterministic doctrine, is a self-deceiver.» The inauthentic life is that which «seek(s) to hide from itself the wholly voluntary nature of existence and its complete freedom.» Conversely, the authentic person is he who actively wills freedom, «that man . . . whose existence precedes his essence . . . who cannot, in any circumstances but will his freedom,» and who therefore cannot but will the freedom of others.[20]

The character in the story who most obviously reflects the concept of inauthenticity is Sonny's brother. His whole life is an elaborate structure of false props, based on exclusion of large hunks of reality, and erected in panicky pursuit of that bourgeois chimera «safety.» Incapable of facing the terror of Sonny's life, he says: «I was dying to hear him tell me he was safe.» Constantly, he dodges reality. He does not want to believe that Sonny is being destroyed, or to know how he must feel: «I didn't want to believe . . .,» «I certainly didn't want to know,» «I guess it's none of my business.» Whenever the dark forces with which Sonny is involved threaten his carefully constructed illusion of safety, he panics. A fear that feels like «a great block of ice» settles in his belly. The idea of Sonny preferring the bohemian life-style of the artist to a respectable career, or jazz and the blues to classical music, arouses in him vehement reactions of fear and anger that clearly betray anxieties beyond brotherly love and solicitude. In his puritan and middle-class mind, black music is associated with intimate knowledge of the realities of existential chaos and absurdity.

Ultimately, what the narrator's anger conceals, is his guilty failure to stop deceiving himself and to heed his mother's words that «Safe, hell! Ain't no place safe for kids, nor nobody.» It is hardly accidental that he is forever watching life through windows: subway windows, classroom windows, cab windows, and living-room windows. His is a life of noninvolvement and detachment behind a fragile glass structure liable to crack or break at any moment. The only advice he is able to offer his brother is derived from the clichés he has adopted from the bourgeoisie he is aping: «I wanted to talk about will power and how life could be — well beautiful.» In short, self-reliance and the sure reward of virtuous living. The algebra he teaches is an accurate symbol of the kind of orderly and predictable world he attempts to establish for himself. Seeking refuge in a «safe» profession, a conventional marriage — the safety of which is ironically negated by the sudden death of his daughter — and conventional ideas, Baldwin's narrator consistently avoids facing «the voluntary nature» of existence, thereby denying freedom not only to himself but to Sonny as well. He commits what in Sartre's terms is the ultimate sin, the very hallmark of inauthenticity: willed self-deception.

On the other hand, Baldwin's black musician-hero lends himself to description in positive existentialist terms. This is not to say that Sonny is reducible to a simple set of philosophical abstractions. In the same way that his brother's evasions are in part responses to his need to escape suffering and degradation, Sonny's acts stem from his need to break the drug habit and avoid self-destruction. Knowing the precariousness of human life in the ghetto, they are involved in real, down-to-earth problems of survival that are part of the story's fictionally established social illusion.

Within this framework of racial and social realism, however, Sonny is endowed with a peculiar charisma and insight into the nature of human existence. A clear indication that Sonny is meant to carry philosophical-ideological meaning is the repeated emphasis on the mythic dimension of his character. Isabel confesses that having Sonny in the house wasn't like living with a person at all. He is not so much a flesh-and-blood human person as «god . . . a monster.» It is as though he is «all wrapped up in some cloud, some fire, some vision all his own.» He is beyond reach, a mystical «presence» or force. The nightclub is his «kingdom» where «his veins bore royal blood.» From the beginning, his peculiar «privacy» is insisted upon. He moves in a world all his own, a solitude in which he is supremely alone with his «visions.» While he is performing, his fellow players are seen gathering around him on the stage as if offering up prayers to him: «Every now and then one of them seemed to say, amen.» No doubt, Baldwin is at pains to establish Sonny as a vehicle expressing a vision of human life, a type embodying truth beyond the literal and specific problems in which he is involved. In several important respects, Sonny comes as close to Absurd Man as any American literary hero of the 1950s. Such concepts as Dread (Angst), nausea, alienation, and absurd freedom sum up his isolated stance as outsider-hero with considerable accuracy.

His disenchantment with America and its discredited Christian cosmology has begun at an early age. At fourteen «he'd been all hipped on the idea of going to India.» He is attracted to Oriental mysticism and the true spirituality of «people sitting on rocks, naked, in all kinds of weather . . . and walking barefoot through hot coals and arriving at wisdom.» The Western myths of rationalism and automatic evolutionary progress are rejected in favor of subjective quests for personal truths and static or cyclic concepts of time. In a letter he writes his brother, he states explicitly his religious apostasy: «I wish I could be like Mama and say the

Lord's will be done, but I don't know it seems to me that trouble is the one thing that never does get stopped and I don't know what good it does to blame it on the Lord.» The educational system has nothing to offer. Nothing in it corresponds with his perception of reality:«I ain't learnt nothing in school. . . . Even when I go.» Eventually he drops out.

But his disillusionment goes deeper than any specific grievances he may have against society. The meaninglessness he feels at the sight of the big-city jungle that surrounds him has its roots in an awareness that human existence itself is dislocated. The «vision all his own» that he has had in his solitude is a vision of the irreconcilible divorce between man and his world. In prison, he has experienced the palpable reality of Nothingness: «I feel like a man who's been trying to climb up out of some deep and funky hole.» He has discovered the ludicrous indecency of human suffering. Watching the revival meeting in the street, he experiences anew the nihilist's revulsion for the universe: «. . . listening to that woman sing, it struck me all of a sudden how much suffering she must have had to go through. . . . It's repulsive to think that you have to suffer that much.» He has encountered «the roar rising from the void,» and he has felt that nauseous «storm inside.» Playing the blues means facing it again and again as he «leave(s) the shoreline and strike(s) out for deep water,» every time running the risk of «drowning in it.» This experience generates in him a feeling of the unreality of reality: «It was that they weren't real,» accompanied by a feeling of utter estrangement from it all, including his own self: «I can't forget — where I've been. I don't mean just the physical place I've been, I mean where I've *been*. And *what* I've been. . . . I can't really talk about it. Not to you, not to anybody. . . . I was all by myself at the bottom of something, stinking and sweating and crying and shaking, and I smelled it, you know? *my stink*. . . .»

What Sonny is haltingly, stumblingly trying to convey in words and imagery of chaos, disorder, and nothingness is ultimately Kierkegaard's «sickness unto death,» Sartre/Roquentin's «nausea,» and Camus/Meursault's experience of absurdity and unreality.[21] In the final analysis, Sonny is the ego recoiling passionately from the human condition, opposed to it by his whole consciousness and instinctual urge toward order and familiarity. It is not fear that he experiences, but Angst — that self-generating, abysmal dread when confronting *le grand néant*. He has become Absurd Man doomed to living, in Camus's phrase, «without appeal.» He has discovered the truth about the «wholly voluntary nature of existence,» life as total possibility, total freedom, total responsibility. Indeed, he has realized that «existence precedes essence,» that there is no preordained human nature, that identity is created by the self through its choices and acts. In Camus's terminology, he is a «metaphysical rebel» whose insurrection is ultimately bound to dispute «the ends of man and creation.»[22] The human condition is perceived as fundamentally unintelligible, which explains his statement that it is the instinct of any man who has looked into the naked terror of an absurd universe to resort to any means to repress the truth «in order to keep from shaking to pieces.»

It is significant that at no time does Sonny feel guilty about his absurdist vision: «I'm not talking about it now because I feel *guilty* or anything like that — maybe it would be better if I did, I don't know.» Sonny's words here are a near-verbatim echo of Camus: «(Absurd Man) does not understand the notion of sin. . . . An attempt is made to get him to admit his guilt. He feels innocent. To tell the truth that is all he feels — his irreparable innocence.»[23] To Sonny's brother there is something almost offensive about such a view of life. To him life is a rational and antitragic affair in which prudence and hard work will open the gate to the life of respectability and security he seeks. Sonny's ideas appear to his black bourgeois imagination the result of pride. Therefore he attempts to impose upon Sonny a feeling of guilt by pointing out how «unreasonable» he is. For Sonny to pursue his vision is labeled a «sin» against Isabel's desire to live respectably, a «sin» against himself trying to make it in society, and even a violation of the memory of their dead mother. These charges fall outside Sonny's frame of reference, however. Sonny's «irreparable innocence» cannot conceive of any such notion of sinfulness and criminality.

It gradually dawns on the narrator that Sonny's music grows out of a valid existential experience. Being told by Isabel's relatives about the fanaticism with which Sonny practices, he realizes that the music is «life or death» to him. His «education» is completed in the Greenwich Village nightclub when he discovers that Sonny's «tale» is not just his own personal story, or the story of his race's trials and tribulations, but that «this tale . . . has another aspect in every country, and a new depth in every generation.» The blues revive memories not only of the troubles of «that long line,» but also of the death, that had nothing to do with race, of his little daughter from polio. Sonny's message expands into the timeless tale of human suffering, of the irrationality and sheer contingency of existence, and of the «freedom that lurked about us.» Describing the impact of the music on the audience and on himself, he feels that it hits something in him, and he senses the growing mood of «apprehension» as Sonny and Creole begin to «tell us what the blues were all about.» Thus what the music does is to create in the presumably interracial audience an experience of existential anguish and a heightened awareness of life as total freedom: «Freedom lurked around us and I understood, at last, that he could help us be free, if we would listen, that he would never be free until we did.» For Sonny, as for Camus's metaphysical rebel, the reason for his inner freedom is the knowledge that there is no future. Like Sisyphus endlessly pushing the boulder back up to the top of the hill, he is doomed to playing the blues. His life must be a life in the present, an indefinite succession of blues acts paradoxically bestowing upon him the same modicum of freedom that Sisyphus enjoys. Sonny's freedom lies in his awareness of the nature of existence, and it is this awareness that liberates him to live to the maximum here and now. The meaning of his life is in the struggle itself. As with Sisyphus, one must imagine Sonny happy.

Defining the blues in terms close to the existentialist sensibility, Ralph Ellison states:

> The blues is an impulse to keep the painful details and episodes of a brutal experience alive in one's aching consciousness, to finger its jagged grain, and to transcend it, not by the consolation of philosophy but by squeezing from it a near-tragic, near-comic lyricism. As a form, the blues is an autobiographical chronicle of personal disaster expressed lyrically. . . . Their attraction lies in this, that they at once express both the agony of life and the possibility of conquering it through sheer toughness of spirit. They fall short of tragedy only in that they provide no solution, offer no scapegoat but the self.[24]

This description fits Baldwin's Sonny to a remarkable degree. His music is nothing if not «an autobiographical chronicle of personal disaster expressed lyrically» and thereby made representative of the lot of all men. The extent to which it is a self-transcending endeavor is suggested by the elaborate ritualization surrounding the concert, from the solemnly «ceremonious» appearance of the players on the bandstand to the subtle interaction between the soloist, the group, and the audience. The performance is metaphorically represented as a progressive movement away from the safe shoreline out into deep water, punctured only by voices whispering «amen» as new mysteries are revealed. They all gather around Sonny as their priest-shaman, vicariously facing the void through him and his music, and partaking of the freedom he is able to wrestle from it by «imposing order on it.» The last stage of the narrator's development, especially his final act of sharing a sacramental drink with his brother, is modeled on the pattern of baptism. Holy Communion, and initiation. The effect of this ritualization is to make Sonny's art a public act and a communal experience to be shared. In the final scene, Sonny becomes the bard and the truth-sayer of all mortals. Acting as their voice and mediator, he is assigned the public function of officiating at a communal ritual of exorcism. Darkness is momentarily pushed back, the forces of destruction appeased. Riding on the waves of Sonny's artistically ordered sound, they enjoy a common triumph, however short-lived, over chaos. Ultimately, then, Baldwin's black musician has transcended both his private destiny and his role as a racial voice to become the modern existentialist Isolato speaking, «on the lower frequencies,»[25] for all human beings. Before the fact of absurdity, all racial and personal distinctions fade away, and the blues become the tragic song of all men.

This is the trans-racial Sonny the story has been straining toward all along, and the underlying ideological requirements motivating Baldwin's character portrayal have already been hinted at. That such an interpretation is not wholly arbitrary is demonstrated by a recent short story by Sam Greenlee that is an explicit rebuttal of «Sonny's Blues» on ideological grounds.[26]

Coming out of the new mood of blackness and celebration of racial solidarity among the post-Wright-Ellison-Baldwin generation, «Sonny's Not Blue» is designed to counteract what the

author sees as the spirit of «white» individualism, integrationism,
and defeatist resignation in Baldwin's story. Greenlee's Sonny is
firmly anchored in the community and his actions subject to
scrutiny by the group. Faced with the necessity of doing better in
school, he does not, like his namesake of fifteen years before, drop
out, but receives the full support of his racial group who actively
encourage him to improve himself so that his achievement will reflect favorably on the whole group. All the blacks in Sonny's
housing project feel and act as one family. Whenever the welfare
checks arrive late, the principle of group cooperation and solidarity starts operating. There are communal celebrations every time
someone stops conking their hair and starts wearing a «'Fro.»
They all stick together in manipulating the welfare agency. The
«white» Standard English insisted upon by the school system is rejected in favor of Black English. Healthy, unpolluted food is ea-
ten. Sonny's mother is no meek praying woman scrubbing the
white folks' floors, but a proud, resourceful person who takes
Sonny to concerts at the Afro-Arts Theatre. The milk he drinks is
«Joe Louis milk,» and when he dreams of buying his mother a
color television set, it is for the purpose of enabling her to watch
the black color of Aretha Franklin's skin.

The spirit of the story is in deliberate contrast to «Sonny's
Blues.» The virtues of blackness are extolled. The social life of the
group seems patterned on African-style village communism in
which the individual has no life apart from the tribal family and
where individual ambition finds its fulfillment within the context
of the group. In contrast to the defensively struggling loner in
Baldwin's story, Greenlee's black characters realize themselves
through racial solidarity and collective action. His Sonny is
emphatically *not* «blue.» Reclaimed by his Afro-American tribe,
he is not tainted by the spirit of resignation and decadent despair
in which Baldwin's «whitewashed» Sonny, cut off from his tribal
roots, permits himself to indulge. Seen from Greenlee's ideological
standpoint, Baldwin's existentialist hero is anathema to the needs
of the black cause in the 1960s and '70s. Even in his most assertive
moments, he appears curiously defensive. His triumphs are
temporary. Although he is provided with the privilege of a usable
racial past and a sense of community, the value of these resources
is heavily restricted. The usable part of his past is limited to the

black urban experience, the Southern folk culture being dismissed
by Sonny as «that old-time, down-home crap.» For all his discovery of a racial community, he remains the solitary individual
going it alone. History and the group are recognized as resources,
but they can only be of help in enduring the paralyzing feeling of
absurdity that is a symptom of white decadence in the first place.
From the point of view of the *engagé* black literature of recent
years, Baldwin's vision is too pessimistic, individualistic, and
white-oriented to be acceptable.

Thus, ironically, the very qualities that were meant to prove
Sonny's universal humanity and modernity, and hence his equality
with the white man, were what made him most offensive in the
eyes of the next generation of black writers. What Sonny proved
to Greenlee and Kelley in the 1960s was not his equality with
whites in a commonly shared humanity, but his author's submission to the allegedly decadent values of a decaying Western
civilization. The ideological situation confronting the black
community and the black writer in the post-civil-rights era was to
require an esthetic and a conception of literary character very
different from those that produced Baldwin's musician-hero.

2.

Constantly making their way into Kelley's fictional world are the
echoes of the civil rights revolution, *soul,* and the black
nationalism of the 1960s. *Dancers on the Shore* is a transitional
collection, reflecting the tensions of the decade. The author's preface, referred to above, indicates the conventional moral and esthetic premise from which he started out, but it can hardly be said
to apply to all the stories in the volume. In some of them, a note of
growing militancy is clearly discernible. The specific targets of
such stories as «Connie» and «A Visit to Grandmother» would
seem to be the black bourgeoisie, and it is not difficult to recognize
in «The Servant Problem» an early version of the first pages of the
«Opal»-section of *dem* (1967), the novel that is Kelley's most
explicit satire of white America to date.

The points of juncture between literature and ideology in «Cry
for Me» are particularly clearly visible in the range of characters

inhabiting the story. White people are an amorphous mass, either parading their opulence at Carnegie Hall concerts or producing their pathetic mass entertainment within the racist conventions of the antebellum plantation tradition. The lightskinned or «yellow» black is discredited by association with sexual perversion and a phoney relationship to black folklore. The urban black — typified by the narrator — is also castigated for his willing adoption of the vices of the decadent city, alienated from race and folk, and immersed in the cheap popular mass culture of contemporary America. By contrast, the dark unadulterated *soul* Negro of Southern rural background, steeped in the folklore of his racial group is celebrated and mythologized to an extent that strongly suggests concerns on the author's part beyond strictly literary creation.

Kelley's presentation of Uncle Wallace makes him a figure of romantic romance. Such figures are, in the words of Marius Bewley discussing Jay Gatsby, «mythic» characters «insofar as they express destinies, aspirations, attitudes typical of man or particular groups. . . .» They are «impersonal» with no distinction between their public and private lives, existing «for the inspection and instruction of the race.»[27]

This description fits Kelley's musician-hero remarkably well. His private life story is as uninteresting as Gatsby's. Wallace has, in fact, no private life, no meaning or destiny as an individual. A completely unself-conscious character, he makes sense only in relation to the racial group. His primary function is public and symbolic: that of embodying tensions and trends alive in the culture, and of symbolizing a new mythos.

Kelley goes even further than Baldwin in creating a mythic halo around the musician-hero. Unlike Sonny, Wallace is not individualized. Psychologically, he has neither depth nor complexity. Next to no information is given to provide him with a realistic past or social context. His life prior to his arrival in New York is shrouded in a misty history of heroic ancestors. The implication is that he belongs to a line of strong men, one of whom — his father — has got his almost supernatural feats of physical strength immortalized in one of Wallaces's songs. He is believed by Carlyle to have been «close to eight feet and made of some kind of fireproof metal.» Wallace himself cuts an impressive figure with his «size of a black Grant's Tomb,» punching his brother «square in the chops so he flew back about twenty feet.» The joint work performance of Wallace and his brother equals that of eight ordinary construction workers, and he claims to have sung «from Friday until the next afternoon.»

As befits the mythic hero, Wallace transcends the laws governing the lives of ordinary mortals. His death remains a mystery defying classification in the categories of human knowledge. Standing around the dead body, the doctors can only shake their heads, unable to explain how he died: «Their wasn't a mark on him, but he was dead all right.» Dismissing the case as inexplicable, one of them says: «There is nothing wrong with him, except he's dead.»

The mythic dimension is further reinforced by analogy with heroes of myth and legend. Wallace is a «big voice crying in the wilderness,» suggesting a white wasteland world awaiting the coming of the heraldic voice of *soul.* In the larger context of Kelley's fiction, there is considerable evidence in support of such an interpretation. With increasingly strong emphasis, the saving power of *soul* in a morally bankrupt white culture has been a major emphasis from as far back even as *A Different Drummer.* The only way for the white man's civilization to survive is, in Baldwin's French phrase, to «se négrifier,»[28] or, in the vocabulary of Ishmael Reed's *Mumbo Jumbo,* to surrender to the Dionysian virus of the «jesgrew,» now operating in Euro-American culture.

Although explicitly disclaiming any church affiliations, Wallace is equipped with semidivine attributes setting him apart from his surroundings. Wherever he goes, he generates an atmosphere of religious solemnity. The cabaret in which he performs is appropriately called *The Lantern,* implying the idea of light in a dark world. Entering for the first time, he discovers a light-colored homosexual folksinger faking the emotion of one of Wallace's most highly treasured songs. Outraged at such a sacrilege, Wallace drives the faker off the stage in a way that suggests Christ chasing the money lenders out of the synagogue. His performances produce an awed silence in the audience as the message is communicated. This representation of the scenes of Uncle Wallace's presence as holy ground is further reinforced in the explicit description of his guitar chords as similar to the sound of «an organ in church.»

In, but not of, this world, Wallace exhibits further characteristics normally associated with figures of myth and legend. Thus Carlyle comments that «Uncle Wallace was innocent.» Untainted by the corruption of society, he can only stare blankly and with utter incomprehension at his relative when faced with its strange ways. His guided tour of New York's underworld of sexual perversion is surrounded by vaguely mythic overtones underscoring the heroic purity of his heart. His innocence of technology is no less «mythic.» Unfamiliar with modern recording techniques, he allows a professional folklorist to record all his songs for thirty dollars. Finally, Wallace is totally ignorant of the existence and practices of the show-business establishment. Approached by a concert producer who wants him to perform in Carnegie Hall, he is confused beyond words and turns to Carlyle for an explanation of Mr. Berger's commercial exploitation of art. In every instance, the laughter is directed, not at Wallace, but at the producer's pretentious speech and appearance or at the miserly treatment of the black singer by Francis Mazer, on whose name Kelley makes a pun indicating the intended object of his ridicule.

Wallace's innocence is the radical innocence of the mythic hero. He cannot be contained within the human moral categories of sin, guilt, and forgiveness, or within the worlds of technology, economics, and politics. His innocence and virginity are primordial, raising him to the level of a demigod. In the final scene, he is established as an object of Dionysian celebration and worship in his temple, possessing healing powers of which the audience vicariously partake by touching his body: «The people was rushing toward him. They was all crying and smiling too like people busting into a trance in church and it seems like everybody in the place was going on stage, trying to get near enough to touch him, grab his hand and shake it and hug him and kiss him even.»

An important point is Kelley's association of Wallace with the folk hero John Henry. Besides such externals as Wallace's bulky appearance and herculean strength, other more indirect analogies can be found. The legendary steel driver's racial purity is paralleled by Wallace's dark complexion and Negroid features. As John Henry was said to be capable of breaking the best worker in the country, so Wallace and his brother can outwork eight regular workers. Carlyle reveals that his uncle's white dinner jacket was won in «some kin-a contest driving piles, or cutting wood.» In the film he plays in, Wallace sings «John Henry,» and the narrator makes it clear that of all the songs his uncle sang, he prefers «Cotton Field Blues» and «John Henry.» He returns to the movie theater over and over again to hear the two-minute song number that is the only thing in the film that is not «cardboardy.» The suggested relationship between Wallace and the folk ballad hero is a major clue to the meaning of the story.

With the mythic mode thus established, the problem arises of how to interpret the intellectual and ideological sources of the story's musician-hero. As an artist thoroughly grounded in the tradition of modern American prose writing, Kelley's work frequently suggests the influence of the myth-making imaginations of Faulkner and Hemingway. From a structural and functional point of view, it is tempting to see Wallace as a character patterned on what Philip Young has called the «code hero» in Hemingway's fiction.[29] Like Pedro Romero, he serves to illustrate to Carlyle and the new generation of blacks «wounded» by the decadence of modern urban America «code» that could restore to them a sense of identity and manhood. A Noble Savage to whom his urban nephew, for all his sympathy, can only have the distant, impersonal relationship one has to a symbol or an idol, Wallace bears perhaps a more than casual resemblance to Hemingway's bull-fighter-priest with whom no mortal can be lastingly involved. At no point in the story does Carlyle see his uncle in personal terms as an individual. To him, Wallace is a «voice» speaking with increasingly greater authority and revealing to him the mysteries of his kingdom of blackness.

Wallace is blackness distilled to its pure, primordial state, the incarnation of the unadulterated black identity that LeRoi Jones's Clay Williams feels stirring inside him but never dares to assume fully. To represent this black ur-soul, Kelley uses a pre-Northern Negro in all his presumed cultural and psychic wholeness. In perfect accordance with the ethos and ideology on which he is predicated, he derives his strength not from intellect, but from instinct, passion, and intuition. Or better perhaps, he is uncontaminated by the white Western dualism that reductively imposes upon the dynamic wholeness of human existence such dichotomies as head versus heart, abstract versus concrete, reflection versus action, individual versus group, and art versus life. His behavior is peculiarly unpremeditated. Like Tucker Caliban in Kelley's first novel, Wallace fuses such dualities. Just as Tucker and the other «new Negroes» in *A Different Drummer,* Wallace too acts spontaneously out of some deeply felt and thought inner urge reminiscent of Senghor's idea of the unfragmented African psyche. His coming North was an act of this kind: «He sent us a telegram; there wasn't enough time for him to write a letter because, he told us later, he only decided to come two days before he showed up.» Similarly, his artistic performances are spontaneous, voluntary acts never undertaken for profit or fame, and never perceived as «high art» involving categorization into creator, artistic object, performer, and audience. His concerts are communal moments of sharing in which such categories become meaningless. Wallace's view of art stands in demonstratively clear contrast to the coolly calculating attitude of Mr. Berger, and even Carlyle, who treat Wallace's art as a field of investment, or the attitude of the Carnegie Hall audience who see the concert as a social occasion and as detached enjoyment of an artistic object.

With perfect consistency, Kelley never has Wallace articulate and conceptualize his ontological assumptions, but *live* them. Applying the vocabulary of James Stewart prescribing a new «cosmology» or «reality-model» for the black artist,[30] one might describe Uncle Wallace's vision of the world as implicitly nonscientific and nonmechanical. In terms antithetical to the white, Western conception of reality, the black man conceives of the world as endless becoming, a state of perpetual flux to be embraced and lived rather than divided, arrested, fixed, and preserved. Life is seen as an all-inclusive process of eternal creation through dialectic reconciliation of conflicting forces in which art cannot be singled out as a separate and specialized activity to be cultivated in isolation for its own sake or as exclusive self-expression. Wallace is conceived in the African image of the tribal artist whose art is perishable and recreated each time, integrated into the life of the community to the point of becoming indistinguishable from it. Wallace does not so much produce art objects as he recreates with each musical act the aboriginal black self in communion with the life force itself. In his art, there is no distortion of reality to create illusions of truth. He just picks up his

guitars and plays as the spirit moves him, artlessly and unself-con-
sciously, affirming and celebrating *la force vitale.*

This interpretation receives support from Kelley's own claim
elsewhere that «African writers and most non-Western writers do
not make a separation between art and life. Art and life and politics are all tied together. . . . Our literary tradition is essentially the
African literary tradition. . . . I think that the mythic, the supernatural, tradition is much more the way we think.»[31] Although this
statement was made three years after the publication of *Dancers
on the Shore,* there is little problem in applying it retroactively to
«Cry for Me.» In fact, placed as it is at the end of the volume, this
story foreshadows Kelley's development toward a more explicitly
separatist esthetic in *A Drop of Patience* — also featuring a
musician-hero — and *dem.*

Furthermore, Wallace's *soul* ethos implicitly repudiates the
individualism so highly treasured in the white man's culture.
Coming back to Bewley's description of the mythic hero, one
might describe Kelley's black musician as a character who cannot
be meaningfully defined in terms of a private destiny. In Wallace
the public and the private merge. Emerging out of a family, racial,
and regional past, he lives and plays «for the inspection and instruction of his race,» returning to his ancestral origins in death. In
Carnegie Hall, he instinctively responds to the presence of a group
of fellow blacks in the audience, although they are almost un-
known to him. Bringing them on stage, he integrates them into the
performance as a matter of course and without any sense of distance between them. No mere trick of composition or sentimental
indulgence, this incident would seem intended to symbolize the
natural fusion of individual and group in an imagination untainted by compartmentalized thinking and reductivist formulas.
Wallace's emotional instincts are communal rather than individual, and his fulfilment lies in group involvement rather than in
personal achievement. No ethic of self-made success, based on a
Darwinist social philosophy of the struggle of the self-reliant individual against the restraints imposed by a hostile society, can adequately explain Wallace's achievement. Such «white» concepts are
alien to his black *soul* sensibility.

Implicit in Wallace's «code» and conveyed through analogy
with John Henry is the rejection of industrialism and the machine

inherent in the *soul* ethos. Though a perennial theme in American intellectual history, Kelley's idea here, or at least the impetus to use it, is more fruitfully related to African or Afro-American ideological currents in the 1960s. It should be noted, however, that his use of folklore is too sophisticated to land him in a reactionary agrarianism simplistically and programmatically dismissing modern industrial civilization. All the time moving on the level of myth, he is able to score his points and avoid any criticism that might come from too literal readings of the story. The symbolic steam drill that forces the steel driver to perform almost supernatural feats of strength is as much Wallace's enemy as it was John Henry's. It suggests a monstrous force mercilessly subjecting men to inhuman ends in the interests of profit and productivity. An agent of chaos and disruption, it implies a denial of the harmonious unity of man and his natural environment. Its predatory nature thrusts upon men in society a competitiveness that separates them and drives them apart. The counterpart to the steam drill in Kelley's story is the New York City with which Wallace engages in a mythic struggle with his guitar and voice and that he ultimately conquers in spite of his physical death. The city's victory is a Pyrrhic one. After the destruction of the body, Wallace's black soul goes marching on, as reflected in the urban Carlyle's gradual awakening to the truths of his uncle's message.

Another implication of the *soul* ethos that Kelley is able to communicate through analogy with John Henry is the alleged sexual superiority of the Negro. Greatly helped by Norman Mailer's «The White Negro,» recent black nationalism has frequently tended to embrace the traditional white myth of the Negro's superior virility, turning it into a counter-mythology with connotations of black sexual superiority. A famous statement of this counter-mythology is Eldridge Cleaver's *Soul on Ice,* which includes explicit laudatory references to Mailer's essay with accompanying diatribes against blacks who, like James Baldwin, refuse to accept Mailer's thesis and are therefore liable to charges of racial self-hatred. Similar overtones can be discerned in the other literary genres, and they have been noted by the anthropologist Roger D. Abrahams who writes that «'Soul' has a sexual dimension to its meanings. . . . Soul has . . . become a euphemism for sexual drive.»[32]

Kelley first alerts us to this aspect of his hero through Carlyle's words that «the most important thing about him was that he wasn't some guy singing about love who never loved, or hard work who never worked hard, because he done all that, loved women and picked cotton and plowed and chopped trees.» The analogy with the ballad hero reinforces this impression through the obvious Freudian implications of John Henry's story. In the words of Richard M. Dorson: «The steel-driver shaking the mountains is a phallic image; singers know that John Henry died from love-making, not over-work:

> This old hammer — *WHAM!*
> Killed John Henry — *WHAM!*
> Can't kill me — *WHAM!*
> Can't kill me — *WHAM!*

Thus the hammer song vaunted the sexual virility of the pounder.»[33]

Wallace is a far cry from the Mailerian idea of the Negro as a healthy psychopath, the counterpart to Colin Wilson's charismatic outsider: the natural existentialist and forerunner of the hipster type, denied «the sophisticated inhibitions of society» and forced to develop a countercultural life-style in which sexual performance became the primary value and the highest art. For all the intensity of his rhetoric, Mailer's black hipster remains a rather helpless abstraction, more effective for what it betrays about the author's despair in a bourgeois intellectual-puritanical culture than for anything it expresses about the black condition. Kelley's Wallace has no need to flaunt his sexual prowess. The point about his superior virility is made through allusion to and analogy with the celebrated sexual powers of one of his racial ancestors. Unobtrusively, the author suggests a continuity between John Henry and Wallace while simultaneously intimating that this is a black asset.

Finally, *soul* harks back to the Southern experience. This embracing on Kelley's part of the Negro's folk roots runs counter to the rejection or, at best, ambivalence, that has traditionally characterized the black bourgeoisie. This middle-class hostility to Southern folk culture has been analyzed by such scholars as Harold Cruse and E. Franklin Frazier,[34] and has received fictional treatment in the works of Charles W. Chesnutt, Jean Toomer, and later writers. A more oblique, but no less revealing statement of the same ambivalent feelings is the exchange between the white critic Stanley Edgar Hyman and Ralph Ellison in 1958.[35] Ellison, following Hyman's attempt to locate the sources of the role-playing trickster archetype in the tradition of blackface minstrelsy, makes a heroic effort to disclaim the trickster's black origin by establishing him as a white American archetype originating with the Revolutionary War and the birth of the Republic, which created the need for role-playing and masks as a substitute for an as yet nonexistent national identity. Ellison's eagerness to avoid association of the negative connotations of the trickster with the Negro can be seen as an indication of the frustrated attitude of the black middle-class intellectual toward his folk past, even as he professes to embrace it and use it in his own work.

Kelley's story lends itself readily to interpretation in terms of the growing pride in the Negro's Southern folk roots in the 1960s. In *A Different Drummer* and *Dancers on the Shore* the author — himself a Northern, urban black — returns to the Southern heritage both for materials and for *soul* with which to infuse them. Uncle Wallace is no primitive Southern black duped by the wicked ways of the big city. His career in New York is cast in the form of a crusade with unadulterated moral and spiritual strength triumphing over decadent sophistication. Described with deliberate absence of realistic detail, the Southern background acquires mythic overtones of heroic loving, singing and working against a suggestively vague tableau of floods and natural disasters inspiring men to herculean feats of strength. Out of this mythic mist Wallace emerges to conquer the city with which he engages in battle. In the present age, the challenges to black *soul* strength are not the natural forces his father fought, but the more insidious forces of New York's phoney «yellow» blacks, the «high» culture of Mr. Berger and the Carnegie Hall crowd, and the commercial movie industry with its «cardboardy» antebellum notions of the Southern planter aristocracy. Fortunately, the symbolic confrontation of the city and the rural past does not degenerate into a simplistic agrarian fantasy. Carlyle survives, and there is every indication that the young black narrator will remain in the city, applying his uncle's message in a modern urban setting. Nor is his «conversion» a naive, adolescent hero admiration, but a reluctant and gradual insight, remaining somewhat inconclusive as the story ends. At the same time, it is clear that through his Southern relative, Kelley's contemporary urban Negro *has* found a viable myth by which to live in a world of urban complexity.

The above should indicate the debt owed by Kelley to some of the central assumptions and ramifications of the Afro-American *soul* ethos in his use of the black musician as literary hero. Wallace is *soul* made visible and elevated to the level of a mythic construct for the use of the race. The further implication is that the new black ethos possesses revitalizing virtues of which contemporary America stands in great need. In several scenes, Uncle Wallace may come close to the brink of notions of the black man's innate superiority, but Kelley manages through an ultimately interracial perspective and Carlyle' realism to stop short of active advocacy of narrowly racialist implications. However strenuously the story exerts itself to assert the unquenchable spirit of blackness, the author avoids indulgence in a sentimental mystique. Wallace is firmly anchored in American culture. He is no exiled African entertaining romantic notions of returning to the Mother continent. Wallace's roots are in the South, just as Carlyle's are in the modern American city. Nor is there an exclusive insistence on narrowly separatist notions of racial self-sufficiency. Wallace will play for any audience, black, white, or interracial, and the ultimate goal of his black folk art is to humanize his fellow men irrespective of race, creed, or color: «He'd taken all them people, and sung to them, and made them forget who they was, and what they come from, and remember only that they was people.» The impact of the music is the same on everybody in the audience. Attempting to articulate the gut effect of Wallace's voice through metaphorical equation with violent stomach pains or sexual orgasm, Carlyle speaks for the whole interracial audience without making any special claims for an exclusive black sensitivity to the truths of *soul,* inaccessible to others. In the «church» of his performances, the musician-priest is black, but he ministers equally to the needs of everybody. The same impression is conveyed in his first novel where Kelley buttresses his case for the black Tucker Caliban's moral and spiritual independence by supportive allusions to Thoreau's *Walden* and Shakespeare's *The Tempest.*

Through such allusions, the author links the virtues of his hero's
black ethos to valuable elements in the Euro-Amesrican heritage in
much the same way that Ishmael Reed's *Mumbo Jumbo* integrates
the black «jesgrew» life-style into an all-inclusive philosophy of
history in terms of the Dionysian principle in Western culture. The
vision emerging from such a broad awareness is impressive indeed,
and one can only regret that in *dem* Kelley shows symptoms of
backsliding into a more narrowly based racial mystique.

Another measure of Kelley's artistic control is the realism built
into the use of point of view. Counterbalancing the story's
straining toward myth and symbol is the narrator's urban, prag-
matic imagination through which everything is filtered. The point
of view restricts the reader to Carlyle's perception of his uncle.
Ultimately then, what we observe is the process of mythmaking in
the narrator's sceptical mind as he grows from seeing his uncle as a
relative to an awareness of him as a force, a symbol and, eventually, a full-fledged myth. This process is gradual and reluctant,
and not entirely completed. Immersed in the white-dominated secular mass culture of the big city, he has dissociated himself from
fertile contact with the cultural roots of his race to the point of all
but losing his capacity for spiritual perception. He feels ashamed
of Southern blacks whom he sees as «all bulgy-eyed and confused,» and of Uncle Wallace on Times Square or at his first performance at The Lantern. His descriptions of his uncle frequently
carry a note of impatience and condescension. He does not «dig»
the folk music or the blues, and «John Henry» in particular is in-
comprehensible: «What an idiot this John Henry must-a been, killing his-self to beat a machine when he could-a joined a union, like
my old man's, and made twice the money and kept the machine
out.» It is clear that at first he cannot grasp Wallace as a symbol.
When a newspaper story establishes Wallace as a «voice speaking
for all the colored folks» and communicating «the pain of
discrimination and segregation,» this seems to Carlyle «like a lot
of B-S . . . because I didn't understand Uncle Wallace hardly myself; I didn't understand why he sang folk songs when he could
sing rock-and-roll or jazz.»

By the end of the story, however, Carlyle has come a long way
toward seeing the significance of Uncle Wallace and accepting him
as a viable myth by which to live. Kelley's choice of a name for his

narrator-character indicates the direction of this characteristically modern transformation of sensibility. Like his namesake in nineteenth-century London, the urban Carlyle in the story is a modern sceptical mind whose latent religiosity takes the form of seeing great men as mythic presences in history and the potential source of a renewed spiritual vision in a secular, materialistic, and utilitarian culture. The symbolism of the name also suggests the author's wish to avoid racial exclusionism, especially if extended by association to the democratic and egalitarian thought of Ralph Waldo Emerson, the British Carlyle's ardent American follower. Such an extension receives further support from Kelley's well-attested affinity with the Transcendentalism of Concord, directly reflected in the title of his first novel.

However, employing the device of dramatic irony, the author does not permit his narrator to grasp the full meaning of the musician-hero. Carlyle's initiation, however genuine, stops short of full adult, conscious understanding, which can be explained both on grounds of psychological credibility and esthetic logic. By withholding full awareness from his narrator, Kelley escapes the mistakes of Sherwood Anderson and Salinger in failing to provide their adolescent narrators with adequate moral and intellectual capacity by making them too young to carry the burden of their stories.In «Cry for Me,» the full import of the story is ultimately contained in the ironic discrepancy between the storyteller's partial vision and the larger vision of the reader. Rather than having Carlyle see, understand, and spell it all out, the author has chosen to leave a richly suggestive slice of reality to be acted upon directly by the reader's imagination.

3.

Pursuing O. Mannoni's and George Lamming's intriguing suggestion that the relationship between Prospero and Caliban in *The Tempest* can be read as a paradigm of the relationship between ruler and subject in a colonialist society, Janheinz Jahn has explored the possibility that Caliban might refuse to remain imprisoned within his master's prescriptive definition of the language he has been taught.[36] To be sure, he will always remain de-

pendent on Prospero's language, and he will always understand
his master's use of it. But Caliban might discover that his culture is
not confined to the colonist's books, and that the magic powers
and the magic knowledge possessed by his native tribe constitute a
valid and legitimate culture even though Caliban can only invoke
it in images. Once he has discovered and self-consciously claimed
this heritage, he may start minting a new language out of
Prospero's imported words and concepts. For all its superficial
resemblance with the original, Caliban's derivation will be a new
and unique creation that can only be partially grasped by the
master and of which he is constantly in danger of missing essential
meanings. The slave will have created a new medium of his own,
no longer identical with the one he was once taught. Caliban will
have broken Prospero's hold on him while continuing to understand Prospero's language.

As they reveal themselves in their respective stories, Baldwin
and Kelley provide illustrative examples of the black American
Caliban in various stages of his development toward a new racial
and cultural self-consciousness and consequent adoption of the
white Prospero's language for his own uses. In «Sonny's Blues,»
the author is Caliban expanding Prospero's framework by in-
fusing it with the magic of his particular island. And yet, for all his
familiarity with the blues, Sonny's ultimate source is to be found
in Prospero's culture. Baldwin's hero is a Euro-American existentialist dressed up as a black blues musician. Denouncing Louis
Armstrong's art as «that old-time, down-home crap,» he reveals
that he has no use for his folk roots in the South. His relationship
with the black community in the North is also somewhat ambivalent. While seeking to identify with it through the music, he is
nevertheless trying to escape it. Baldwin leaves Sonny playing not
in Harlem among his own people, but in Greenwich Village to an
interracial audience. This is not denying either the authenticity or
the validity of Baldwin's portrait of the black musician as existentialist, but the point should be reiterated that in the final analysis the emphasis is on Sonny's existentialism rather than on his
blackness. On the background of the urgently felt need to secure
acceptance and integration of the race in the first postwar decade,
Baldwin's story dramatizes — beyond its autobiographical elements and purely narrative logic — the strategy of the black intelli-

gentia of seizing upon a white concept in order to «negrify» it and pass the hybrid off as a symbol of a commonly shared humanity.

Kelley's strategy in the following decade was to reverse this process, as should be expected from a Caliban in a more advanced stage of racial self-consciousness. Starting with an image of the aboriginal black self still extant on the Afro-American island, this author exploits the resources of Prospero's Christian symbolism, Freudian psychology, and ideas of literary art to project a hero who, for all his analogy with a Hemingway «code hero» or a Faulknerian myth, remains a black magician. Essentially, Wallace is *soul* energy, claimed and appropriated through the language and concepts he was once taught and that he has now refashioned. He is Caliban after he has broken out of his master's prison.

Kelley, however, has not succumbed to the temptation of making Caliban's experience inaccessible to the white American Prospero. The goal of Wallace's art is to humanize everybody in the audience and to make them conscious of their common humanity. This is not to be confused, however, with the traditional pleading for equality. Equality is automatically assumed with Wallace being offered as a symbol of a revitalizing ethos that could lift the curse on the modern American wasteland. The responsibility of answering this challenge is placed squarely on the shoulders of the oppressor. But at least the oppressor is deemed worthy of attention.

Notes

[1] Edmund Fuller, *Man in Modern Fiction* (New York: Random House, 1958), p. 7.

[2] Hugh M. Gloster, «Race and the Negro Writer,» in *Black Expression,* ed. Addison Gayle, Jr. (1950; reprint ed., Weybright and Talley, 1969), p. 257.

[3] Collected in James Baldwin, *Going to Meet the Man* (New York: Dell, 1965).

[4] James Baldwin, «Autobiographical Notes,» *Notes of a Native Son* (New York: Bantam, 1964), p. 6.

[5] Significant essays by Césaire, Diop, and Senghor have been collected in *Anthologie Négro-Africaine,* ed. Lilyan Kesteloot (Verviers, Belgium: Gérard & Company, 1967). The concept of *Négritude* has received extensive treatment by Janheinz Jahn in *Neo-African Literature* (New York: Grove Press, 1969). Other critical essays are «Negritude: Literature and Ideology» by Abiola Irele, *Modern*

Black Novelists, ed. M. G. Cooke (Englewood Cliffs, N.J.: Prentice-Hall, 1971), pp. 13-23, and *The Black Militant Writer in Africa and the United States* by Mercer Cook and Stephen E. Henderson (Madison: The University of Wisconsin Press, 1969).

[6] Cook and Henderson, *Black militant writer,* p. 127.

[7] William Melvin Kelley, Preface to *Dancers on the Shore* (Chatham, N.J.: Chatham Booksellers, 1964).

[8] Collected in Kelley, *Dancers on the Shore.*

[9] Marcus Klein, *After Alienation* (New York: Meridian Books, 1972), pp. 172-73.

[10] Shirley Anne Williams, *Give Birth to Brightness* (New York: Dial Press, 1972),pp. 145-46.

[11] Edward Margolies, *Native Sons* (Philadelphia and New York: Lippincott, 1968), p. 107.

[12] Collected in Baldwin, *Notes of a Native Son.*

[13] Esther Merle Jackson, «The American Negro and the Image of the Absurd,» Phylon, 23 (1962): 359-71.

[14] Nathan A. Scott, «Search for Beliefs: Fiction of Richard Wright,» *University of Kansas City Review,* 23 (1966): 19.

[15] Richard Wright, «How Bigger Was Born,» in *Twentieth-Century Interpretations of Native Son,* ed. Houston A. Baker, Jr. (Englewood Cliffs, N.J.: Prentice-Hall, 1972), pp. 21-47. Parts of the article originally appeared in the *Saturday Review of Literature,* 1 June 1940.

[16] Richard Wright, *White Man, Listen!* (New York: Doubleday, 1964), pp. 71-72.

[17] Baldwin, *Notes of a Native Son,* p. 104.

[18] Kenneth Stampp, *The Peculiar Institution* (New York: Random House, 1956), p. vii.

[19] The term is used by George Lukacs in his essay «The Intellectual Physiognomy of Literary Characters,» in *Radical Perspectives in Art,* ed. Lee Baxandall (1936, reprint ed., Harmondsworth: Pelican, 1972), pp. 89-141.

[20] Quoted from Jean-Paul Sartre's *Existentialism and Humanism* (1946) in *The Modern Tradition,* ed. Richard Ellman and Charles Feidelson, Jr. (New York: Oxford Univ. Press, 1965), pp. 842-43.

[21] Søren Kierkegaard, *The Sickness unto Death,* trans. Walter Lowrie (Princeton, N.J.: Princeton Univ. Press, 1941); Jean-Paul Sartre, *La Nausée* (Paris: Gallimard, 1961); Albert Camus, *L'Etranger* (Paris: Gallimard, 1970).

[22] Albert Camus, *The Rebel* (Harmondsworth: Penguin, 1962).

[23] Quoted from Camus's *The Myth of Sisyphus* (1942), in *The Modern Tradition,* p. 845.

[24] Ralph Ellison, *Shadow and Act* (New York: The New American Library, 1964), pp. 90, 104.

[25] Ralph Ellison, *Invisible Man* (Harmondsworth: Penguin, 1965), p. 469.

[26] Sam Greenlee, «Sonny's Not Blue,» collected in *Black Short Story Anthology,* ed. Woodie King (New York: Columbia Univ. Press, 1972).

[27] Marius Bewley, «Scott Fitzgerald's Criticism of America,» *Twentieth-Century Interpretations of The Great Gatsby,* ed. Ernest Lockridge (1954; reprint ed., Englewood Cliffs, N.J.: Prentice-Hall, 1968), pp. 40, 44.

[28] Interview with *L'Express,* August 21-27, 1972, p. 69.

[29] Philip Young, *Ernest Hemingway* (New York: Rinehart, 1952).

[30] James Stewart, «The Development of the Black Revolutionary Artist,» *Black Fire,* ed. LeRoi Jones and Larry Neal (New York: William Morrow & Co., 1968), pp. 3-10.

[31] Quoted in Jervis Anderson, «Black Writing: The Other Side,» *Dissent,* 15 (1968): 236-37.

[32] Roger D. Abrahams, *Positively Black* (Englewood Cliffs, N.J.: Prentice-Hall, 1970), p. 144.

[33] Richard Dorson, «The Ballad of John Henry,» *An American Primer,* ed. Daniel J. Boorstin (New York: The New American Library, 1968), p. 463.

[34] Harold Cruse, *The Crisis of the Negro Intellectual* (New York: William Morrow & Co., 1967); E. Franklin Frazier, *Black Bourgeoisie* (New York: The Free Press, 1957).

[35] «The Negro Writer in America: An Exchange,» *Partisan Review,* 25 (1958): 197-222.

[36] Janheinz Jahn, *Neo-African Literature: A History of Black Writing* (New York: Grove Press, 1968), pp. 239-42, 269.

2

«Desecrators» and «Necromancers»:
Black American Writers and Critics in the 1960s
and the Third World Perspective

To presume to make definitive judgements about the black American literary nationalism of the 1960s is foolhardy. Its critical and creative fruits present themselves to us as shifting and unruly strains in a still ongoing process. The student of contemporary Afro-American writing finds himself wandering, dazed, in a hot-house of artistic growth whose sheer diversity and contrary pulls defy any attempt at confident generalizing.

One possible general perspective on this «neo-black» creativity, however, is to view the new generation as engaged in an enterprise parallel to that of postwar African and Caribbean writers: «a type of reconnaissance in the formation of a new imaginative world free from the proscriptions of a racist West.»[1] To see literary expression by black Americans in the 1960s as a collective effort to create such a new imaginative world is to enter into its innermost spirit. After what was felt to be the bankruptcy of the image that had controlled the first postwar decade — «the Negro as America's metaphor» — this was the revisionist task demanded of a new literary generation: the formation of a new imaginative order purged of oppressive white influence. In realizing this aim, as the decade progressed, black artists in the United States increasingly saw themselves as engaged in an enterprise parallel to what Samuel Allen describes as the task undertaken by Senghor's group in Paris: «to cast off the cultural imprint of colonial Europe.»[2] After 1965 — the year of crossroads for so many — the colonial metaphor to a large extent ruled the new black literary thought. It was these changes of consciousness and sensibility, as they were reflected in the highly publicized real-life models of Malcolm X, Eldridge Cleaver, Frantz Fanon, Stokeley Carmichael, LeRoi Jones/Amiri Baraka, H. Rap Brown, Julius Lester, George Jackson, Angela Davis, and others, that underlay the thrust to establish a new imaginative island that, though in the West, would not be of it.

The formation of such a literary sensibility could not take place in a vacuum, however. Given the recalcitrance of historical experience, it was inevitable that the redefinition of black American identity as a diasporic identity and of black American art in an African or Third World context had to find its specific expression within already familiar categories in New World black writing. Observing the Afro-American literary scene of the 1960s with the benefit of hindsight, one discerns this interaction between the new Third World vistas and traditional black American patterns at work in the transformation of the classic twin impulse in black American letters toward rage and celebration, traditionally expressed in protest writing and in literary tributes to the Negro's redemptive heritage in the American «dusty desert of dollars and smartness» (W.E.B. Du Bois in *The Souls of Black Folk)*. No longer did black poets, dramatists, and prose writers conceive of themselves within the time-honored roles of angry pleaders for Negro rights or celebrators of the quintessential Americanness of the racial experience. In their efforts to de-Westernize black art, this was the new and revised duality: a fiery wrath and, on the other hand, a proud exaltation of an exclusive blackness, a passionate urge to «murder and create.» The result was to recast the black writer in the double role of — in Larry Neal's and Ishmael Reed's African-American terminology — «desecrator» and «necromancer.»

What the present chapter proposes to deal with, then, is this metamorphosis of the traditional pattern of rage and celebration resulting from a compelling desire to repudiate the aesthetic derived from «the-Negro-as-America's-metaphor.» The black man was to be detached from the West and brought into the orbit of the post-Western humanism being forged in the new historical crucible of an Afro-centric Third World. However individual the responses to the meaning and relevance of Africa, the call that issued from the new writing was for a dissociation of black America from the cultures of the First and Second Worlds and a reinterpretation of the racial experience.

In this yearning to attach black America to a cultural matrix outside the Euro-American tradition so as to join in the adventure of shaping a superior post-Western humanism one also sees reflected the profoundly idealistic spirit at the core of the massive release of expressive energy in the latter half of the decade. The specific meaning of that humanism remained rather vague, however. Only tenuously linked to Renaissance and eighteenth century thought, it is more easily understood as a kind of Romantic sensibility. The liberal heritage of the Enlightenment was in fact often virulently attacked on the grounds that it had served as a means to keep blacks docile and dependent on the Western tradition. Its false concepts of rationality and universality were felt to have deprived blacks of the particularity and legitimacy of their culture. Instead they projected an alternative ethos of spontaneity and action, revolt, a Pan-African *Volksgeist* and Afro-American nationhood, and concern for the dispossessed and the downtrodden. In a Euro-American civilization geared to material production, such ideas of human self-realization and *communitas* would forever remain alien. Hence the constructive challenge before the black writer was no longer grafting the black American's soul, as seen through the vistas of nearly four hundred years, on to the tree of his African brother's *negritude* in a shared synthesis of consciousness and sensibility. Only in such a synthesis, forged on the Third World frontier whose vanguard is modern Africa, was a new humanism deemed possible, indispensable not only to the survival and self-discovery of the black American, but to the survival and advancement of all human culture in the embattled global village that is the modern world. The judgements of such a herculean effort will vary. But in judging its success, one should not forget that to set impossibly high goals for the race's literary craftsmen has always been part of the tradition of black American letters. In every generation, demands have been made of it that have imposed burdens not ordinarily imposed on any art.

Such, then, was the new literarily productive sensibility of the second postwar decade, born of the encounter between new geopolitical and historical circumstances and patterns of expression rooted in the soil and experience of the racial group in America. It is into this sensibility that we must now reconnoiter, bearing in mind that what we can hope to discover is no more than the disclosure of a shared intellectual perspective in the midst of contemporary flux.

As the 1950s were drawing to a close, a sense of momentous and impending change in Negro American culture made itself felt among its articulate spokesmen. In the columns of *Phylon,* it found expression in the symbolic use of Matthew Arnold's autobiographical persona in *Stanzas from the Grande Chartreuse,* projected as a wanderer between two worlds, one dead, the other not fully born.[3] In John Lash's and Arthur P. Davis's usage, the reference was to the old world of racial segregation and the rising world of true integration and full participation of the Negro in all areas of national life. Ralph Ellison restated his firmly held belief that America is one and that the whole question of «whether there is a Negro culture might be cleared up if we said that there were many idioms of American culture, including, certainly, a Negro idiom of American culture in the South. We can trace it in many, many ways. . . . But it is American, and it has existed a long time.»[4] Their statements all concurred in their perception of the Negro's essential Americanness and in a shared conviction that his cultural achievement must be understood in New World terms.

In line with the Arnoldian metaphor and with particular reference to Negro writing, established men of letters expressed their sense of a historical watershed in similar terms. Blyden Jackson impressed upon the Negro novelist «the duty and opportunity» to forego the traditional «never-never Cytherea of the Clotel complex, on the one hand, and the romanticizing of a black proletariat, on the other» and to record instead the «growing assimilation of the Negro to the American middle class. . . . This is the middle ground which is a golden mean for the Negro novel in its role as protestant against the exclusion of the Negro from the norms of American life.»[5] And Philip Butcher, surveying recent black fiction at the opening of the new decade, saw grounds for optimism in the fact that the new writers now seemed prepared to abandon old stereotypes in favor of well-documented stories of the Negro's «wider inclusion in the fabric of American life.»[6] Arna Bontemps's intuition of what he saw as «The New Black Renaissance» was keener and on the verge of prophecy. He sensed in the most recent crop of Negro writers a new orientation bearing considerable resemblance to the 1920s and the search for roots that animated the literary life of Harlem in that era. But even Bontemps envisaged the coming flowering of black art as a contribution to the joint corpus of American cultural expression.[7]

However, even as the wanderer toward full Americanization in the imagination of Davis's generation appeared to be materializing before their very eyes, historical ironies were at work that were to give a radically different meaning to Arnold's metaphor as it applied to the new black writing in the 1960s. The geopolitical event that was to catapult their confident predictions and point the literary wanderer toward different horizons was the rise of the colonized Third World, symbolized by the proclamation of a free Ghana under Nkrumah's leadership in 1957.

The cultural and artistic implications of this event soon made themselves felt. Their outward expressions could be observed on such occasions as the formation in 1958 of the American Society of African Culture (AMSAC), a branch of the Paris-based Society of African Culture (SAC) whose official publication, *Présence Africaine,* had been actively promoting *Négritude* among blacks in the Western world since 1948, and in the presence of black American artists and intellectuals at African cultural festivals in Paris and Rome in 1956 and 1959, and in Lagos and Accra in 1960, 1961 and 1962. Another symbolic event was Senghor's visit to the United States in 1962 and the literary luncheon given at the White House in his honor. Africa was rapidly becoming a visible presence to a reluctant Negro literary establishment still presided over by Saunders Redding, Arthur P. Davis, and Blyden Jackson, and whose star writer was the Baldwin who admitted in letters from the journey that was meant to carry him to Africa: «I have a gloomy feeling that I won't find any answers in Africa, only more questions.» Writing from Loche-les-Bains in February 1962, racked by guilt, but incapable of remorse, he stated: «I simply dread facing the tigerish Negro press if I return to America without having visited the land which they so abruptly are proud to claim as home. The more particularly as neither *Another Country* nor my report on Africa is likely to please them at all.»[8] Baldwin on this occasion never made it to Africa at all.

The deeper issues of cultural identity and artistic purpose stirred by the new historical winds and the responses they elicited are conveniently capsulized in the controversy, widely publicized at the time, between Harold Cruse and Saunders Redding over the relevance to black America of the emerging Third World perspective. Printed in *Presence Africaine* in January 1958,[9] Cruse's article «An Afro-American's Cultural View» provokingly asked:

«As Negroes of Afro-American descent, and as writers, artists, creative individuals, whose culture do we develop and uphold — an Afro-American culture or an Anglo-Saxon culture?»

Equating the current colonial liberation with the struggle of the Negro in America, he made a case for the autonomous existence of a distinctive black American culture that, though bearing the indelible stamp of the Negro's experience in the New World, must be defined in terms of its African origins and relation to the present-day awakening of «the colored peoples of the world.» «The American Negro cannot be understood culturally unless he is seen as a member of a detached ethnic bloc of people of African descent reared for three hundred years in the unmotherly bosom of Western civilization.» Exhorting black artists and intellectuals to abandon their traditional «Caucasian idolatry in the arts . . . and immature mimicry of white aesthetics» and to rehabilitate black art through a cultural renaissance analogous to the revival of indigenous cultures accompanying political nationalism in Africa, Cruse sought to establish an entirely new context and a new direction for black American artistic endeavor.

The response of J. Saunders Redding, the acknowledged dean of Negro American letters, was prompt and predictable. Addressing AMSAC's First Conference of Negro Writers in 1959, he mounted a direct attack, printed in the *New Leader* (May 1960),[10] against the basic conception expounded by Cruse of the American Negro minority as a people and a nation with a distinctive and autonomous cultural identity. To distinguish between an «Afro-American culture» and an «Anglo-American culture,» Redding argued, is «not only wrong but wrong-headed. The American Negro people are not a *people* in Cruse's sense of the word» and to posit an analogy between African colonial liberation and the struggle of the American Negro for equal rights reveals «total blindness to the truth.» In Redding's scheme, Negro culture is part and parcel of the mainstream of American experience, its folk culture — including music, dance, and vernacular speech patterns — no less than its formal literature. The latter is as intimately related to general American literature as the bough is to the branch, and the difference is «so slight that to be seen at all it must be pointed out.» The test Redding applied to prove his point was that, with few exceptions, no work by or even about Negroes before 1950 had been widely debated because it was controversial. This was evidence, in Redding's view, that black American writing had in every period conformed to «the prevailing state of the contemporary American mind.» In this fact, too, somewhat paradoxically, he found the only and «subtle distinction» between the two literatures: while sharing the nonaestheticist nature of American literary expression as well as its traditional integration of «high culture» and «popular culture» elements, Negro writing is distinguished by its passive and receiving role vis-à-vis the cultural ideas and values informing it. Historically, its role has never been that of a shaping force, but of a conformer and reflector. Redding saw further corroboration of his view in the absence in Negro American history of anything resembling the Jewish reaction of Zionism to the condition of being disinherited and segregated. In fact, paradoxically, that condition has only served to intensify the Negro's «efforts as a social and literary man. . . toward validating his claim to the American heritage.» The conception that emerges from Redding's thinking is the Baldwinian one of the Negro as a historical tabula rasa whose African roots were brutally and completely severed during slavery and whose hope for an identity could only lie in «appropriating these white centuries.»[11] Consequently, for Redding, to speak of an identity problem for the American Negro artist is a misnomer, and to define him in an African and Third World context is wrong. As suggested in the attack on Cruse, and further elaborated in a later essay, the issue is «much less a problem of identity than of identification.»[12] The matter of the American Negro writer's identity was settled a long time ago. In words that in their abstract ring betray Redding's difficulty in grasping the vivifying potential of the new historical forces for black American creative expression, he depicts the African artist as living in a tribal and religious culture almost untouched by modernization. On this basis, Africa is dismissed as having no direct or immediate relevance to Negro art in America either in terms of cultural self-definition or as a source of aesthetic inspiration. For Redding, the central problem of the Negro writer was and remained that «he is not permitted his identification with American culture.»[13]

But the Trojan horse was already within the citadel. Immediately following Redding's attack on Cruse at the First Conference of

Negro Writers, Samuel Allen delivered his paper entitled «Negritude and Its Relevance to the American Negro Writer.» Though not directly attempting a redefinition of black American literary creativity in a Third World context, Allen nevertheless eloquently affirmed the usability of the African past both on the basis of African retentions in New World black culture and African-American linkages in the postcolonial situation:

> In the historical light of the interaction of cultures, there is no reason why the African heritage may not be a fertile source of inspiration. It will be futile to admonish that our roots are American only, that our roots go back to the Virginian shore in 1619 and stop at the water's edge, amid the branding and the cries and trance-like intonations such as those of Cassandra when carried by Agamemnon back to Greece: «What isle, what land is this?».[14]

Other events and coincidences conspired to remind the black literary community of the new forces at work. At the very time Redding was heading the conservative reaction to the new issues forced on the Negro by postcolonial Africa, *Raisin in the Sun* was playing on Broadway. Hansberry's play marked the first appearance in black American drama of an African intellectual as a major character. An equally significant symbolism, perhaps, was the fact that Asagai's main function in the play was as norm and behavior model for an emasculated Chicago Negro and his young identity-seeking sister. This event was followed by the publication of Langston Hughes's anthology *An African Treasury* and *Freedomway's* special Africa issue.[15] Finally, and compounding these ironies, already before the new decade had been ushered in, the very same metaphor that Davis and Lash had used so confidently to herald the full Americanization of the Negro was showing signs of yielding to the pressures of the new historical tide. In 1959, at the Second Annual Conference of the American Society of African Culture, Harold Isaacs read his paper entitled «The American Negro and Africa.» Isaacs, too, projected the contemporary Negro as moving «in and between parts of two worlds,» but in his vocabulary, the reference was to a new black American who, though still struggling to slough off the old self-hatred stemming from

internalized racist images of primitive «Poplarvilles and Talla-
hasses and the great host of their less visible equivalents,»[16] had
acquired a new self-image derived from a positive identification
with modern Africa.

These initial skirmishes over the relevance of Africa and the
Third World to black America and the intimations that the black
Arnoldian wanderer might be about to begin navigating by new
stars did not lead to immediate and dramatic literary results. Thus,
in his introduction to *An African Treasury,* Langston Hughes
went no further than to suggest certain similarities in the patterns
of issues and reactions found in African and black American
writing. In 1960, the only example of a shared racial consciousness
he could detect in these literatures was a common quality of
«blackness» in the search for roots that he felt typefied both the
Harlem Renaissance and modern African art. The stage of a
deeper redefinition of black American literary expression in terms
of the emerging Third World perspective would only be reached in
the second half of the decade. A leavening period was needed
during which the new vistas that were opening up could mature
and take hold.

As the new decade progressed, two observers showed a special
affinity for the emerging African-American sensibility that in the
latter half of the sixties would yield such exciting literary crops.
Working within a new kind of vocabulary, John Henrik Clarke
and Harold Cruse[17] spoke of a new breed of American Negro, a
new «African-minded Afro-American,» of a black American
«colony» and a black American «nationalism,» and of the «Pan-
African» perspectives in the Negro's situation. By 1962, the .
contours of a new consciousness was crystallizing with sufficient
clarity for Cruse to feel justified in assigning to it a label of its
own: «a new set of political and cultural values which, taken
together, have come to be called «Afro-Americanism»». The specific thrusts behind this «Afro-Americanism,» Cruse argued, were
the sense of a lag in the progress of American blacks toward freedom compared to the advances made in the colonial world, and
the sharpened feeling of isolation and alienation in the West. Also,
the resurgent interest in African affairs among New World blacks
stimulated the awareness of a shared colonial condition.
Distinguishable from previous ideological patterns in Negro his-

tory by its hostility or scepticism toward NAACP's legalism, white liberals, Marxist groups, and the exclusiveness of the Muslims, the temper of the new «Afro-American» outlook could best be gauged, Curse felt, by looking at its «pantheon of modern heroes»: Camus, Lumumba, Nkrumah, Sekou Touré, Castro, Mao Tse-tung, Robert Williams, and Malcolm X. In Cruse's pantheon, black Americans joined hands with Africa, Asia, and the Caribbean in their common historical revolt. «For those who adopt it,» he concluded, «Afro-Americanism serves the purpose of placing them in close rapport with the content and spirit of the world revolution.»

Such were the new vistas whose leavening impact was at work in the first half of the decade. Not until the *crise de conscience* of the mid-sixties, however, did they come to fruition as a basis for literary creativity. Traditional Negro confidence in white liberal ideals was severely shaken after 1965. It was becoming increasingly clear that major legislative victories, including the Civil Rights Act and the Voting Rights Act, would not be sufficient to secure the integration of not just deserving individuals, but the black masses. A mood of rapidly growing disenchantment set in, erupting in urban riots across the nation in a succession of «hot summers.» Black confidence was further weakened by what looked like the gathering momentum of a concerted white backlash at home and abroad. In the ensuing intellectual and ideological vacuum, a radicalization of black literary thought occurred that stimulated separatist ideas. This development was not without precedent in black American history. What was different for literary intellectuals this time, however, was the geopolitical context of a black American cultural revival. The literary scene was ripe for an influx of the ideas that had been incubating for some time and whose implications for black literary expression had been a major concern of the *Négritude* movement and *Présence Africaine* in the whole postwar period.

The writings of black American literary intellectuals in the second half of the decade abundantly reflect their preoccupation with this crisis of consciousness and sensibility leading to identification with an Afro-centric Third World. Their statements were often aglow with the joy of observing the ancestral continent emerge from obscurity on to the global historical arena. In *The*

New Black Poetry, perhaps the most significant anthology of black American verse to come out of the 1960s, Clarence Major's preface spoke of «the inner crisis of black reality,»[18] while Stephen Henderson commented in the apocalyptic rhetoric of the times on the «profound revolution. . . in the minds of black people» that, when completed, will have turned «Negroes» into «black people»,[19] transforming or destroying America in the process. Another characteristic expression of their shared experience of crisis and reorientation is found in Sonia Sanchez's preface to *We Be Word Sorcerers,*[20] an anthology of fiction by twenty-five black American writers of the late sixties. According to the editor's claim, each of the contributors «was born a Negro with no knowledge of himself or history. Each one of us was the finished product of an American dream, nightmarish in concept and execution. Each one of us has survived to begin our journey toward «Blackness.» In the works of these and other writers, the literary journey to «Blackness» followed a variety of routes. Nikki Giovanni's took her from her youthful position as «Ayn Rand-Barry Goldwater all the way»[21] to that of reigning poet of the Black Arts Movement. Baraka went from Ruthers and Howard, the U.S. Air Force, and Greenwich Village to revolutionary writing and politics in Harlem, Newark, and Africa. Yet another pattern is reflected in William Melvin Kelley's career as he moved from the exclusive Fieldstone School and the Harvard English Department to committed racial fiction and residence in Africa and the West Indies.

Animating all these literary odysseys from «Negroness» to «Blackness» was a shared impulse to move beyond the first post-war vision of the black man as America's metaphor and to free Afro-America and her art from the shackles of a declining and antihumanistic civilization by seeking a new anchorage in historically ascending cultures. Major saw his collection of black verse as rooted in a spirituality and a historical sense reaching back beyond Jamestown to the parent continent. In this perspective, the black man's New World experience dwindles in significance to a relatively minor episode whose chief event, Emancipation, is an important reference point only in the white man's fantasy world. In Henderson's vision, William K. Kgositsile — a black American born in South Africa — appeared as a symbol of the new African-

American imaginative world and of a Pan-African literary synthesis spanning both hemispheres. In a passage quoted by Henderson, he expressed this new bicontinental literary sensibility in lyrical prose:

> There is nothing like art — in the oppressor's sense of art. There is only movement. Force. Creative power. The walk of Sophiatown tsotsi or my Harlem brother on Lenox Avenue. Field hollers. The Blues. A Tane riff. Marvin Gaye or mbaqanga. Anguished happiness. Creative power, in whatever form it is released, moves like the dancer's muscles.
> But the impulse is personal.[22]

One specific effect of this Afro-centric thought on black American writing may be observed in its impact on the classic pattern of rage and celebration. In the pre-Civil War period, this duality of expressive modes is found on the one hand in black abolitionist oratory, slave narratives, and, on the other hand, in a rich crop of black jokelore and folktales. At the turn of the century, the same twin impulse may be found embodied in Paul Laurence Dunbar's *The Sport of the Gods* (1902) and in Charles Chesnutt's *The Conjure Woman* (1899). The former is simultaneously a chronicle of the disintegration of a rural black family in the big city and a story of the making of the ghetto, whose bitterness is communicated through the conventions of contemporary naturalistic fiction, as suggested by the title. Chesnutt's sequence of Uncle Julius tales, on the other hand, made extensive use of folk materials to celebrate the resilience and resourcefulness of black folk. Using irony to circumvent the racist stereotypes demanded by white publishers and readers, Chesnutt made his storytelling hero a figure reveling in his blackness and ways of «puttin' on ole massa.» In the literature of the Harlem Renaissance, the same duality appears with almost schematic neatness in the work of Claude McKay and Jean Toomer. The sonnets of McKay, the Jamaica-born «black Prometheus» (Nathan Huggins in *Harlem Renaissance)* whose personal friends included Max Eastman, Floyd Dell, John Reed, and Marcus Garvey, may not have contributed much in the way of technical innovation, but *Harlem Shadows* (1922) did stake out new territory for this time-honored poetic form by the racial and social commitment and violent language of several of its pieces. Conversely, *Cane* was an incantatory celebration of a uniquely black ethos. Through figures of redemptive black womanhood (Fern, Karintha) and the preacher-prophet Barlo, «a clean-muscled, magnificent black-skinned Negro» whose vision of the rise of the «big and black and powerful» African ancestor of all New World blacks inspires supernatural events in the Southern town, Toomer mythologized the unadulterated sensibility of the black folk of Georgia's «Dixie Pikes» in a spirit of racial pride. Finally, post-Renaissance writing may be accommodated within the same historical duality. The Great Depression hit the black community hardest of all, arousing literary anger to a pitch unsurpassed up to that point in the early work of Richard Wright. The antihero of *Native Son* was a confrontation with the accumulated damage inflicted on the black man in America and a release of phobias, anxieties, and aggressions. Following this outburst of anger, a spirit of celebration became the dominant mood as a new literary generation, headed by James Baldwin and Ralph Ellison, emerged in the early 1950s. The peculiar achievement of this generation was to reinterpret the racial experience in the light of postwar existential ideas so as to assign to that experience a priestly and redemptive role in a war-battered and crisis-conscious Western culture.

In black American writing of the 1960s, this duality pesrsisted, but its meaning changed. The change is reflected in the imagery created by a new generation to express the role of the racial artist. Seeing the poetry of the period as permeated by a twin impulse to «murder and create,» Eugene Redmond has described the poetic field as a spectacle of «festivals and funerals.»[23] In the same spirit, Henderson praised Kgositsile's poems as a body of work whose voice «speaks thunders . . . or sings with liquid fire,»[24] and in the introduction to his anthology, Clarence Major described the poems assembled as simultaneously «death cries» to a capitalistic and racist West and «solar concerts to the infinite tacit incantations of our elegance, as we are, as we long to be. Black radiance.» In the many neologisms coined to express the artist's vocation, scattered throughout black writing of the late sixties, the same duality appears. One cluster includes such words as *warrior, fighter, soldier, machine gunner, assassin, hunter, desecrator,* while in the other are found designations of the writer as «necromancer»:

neo-hoodoo soothsayer, conjurer, magician, wizard, babalawo, shaikh, griot, shaman, sorcerer, exorcist, enchanter, and *oracle.* Drawn from Third World anticolonial politics and African tribal backgrounds, such imagery served the purpose of de-Westernizing black American aesthetic thought. At the same time, it was a reenactment of a classic duality in the literary expression of New World blacks.

As the decade progressed, a new generation subjected the accustomed meaning and function of literary anger to severe critical scrutiny. Increasingly, writers abjured traditional protest, finding it corrupted by illusions and false assumptions that they felt invalidated it as a viable mode. In a representative essay entitled «The New Black Literature,»[25] Hoyt Fuller argued that moral evasion is at the core of the protest genre. Western civilization must find some way of assuaging the guilt imposed by its monstrous crimes in our century. In the American context, whites face an imputation of guilt in the very facts of black life. One strategy devised to avoid admission of complicity is manipulation and control of the definition of black literary expression by labeling it «protest literature.» In this way, Afro-American literature may be dismissed, placed in a special category on the periphery of art. This assignment of the black writer to a special province or «ghetto» of literary creation demonstrates the determination of the white majority culture to prevent the minority artist from moving into a position where he can project his own personal and group symbols. Obsessed with controlling this literature in order to relieve their fears and guilt feelings, whites have fashioned a protest formula for use by blacks with ready-made prescriptions for characterization, theme, and plot. It was this formula, with its sinister implications, that Cecil Brown, himself one of the neo-black novelists, described in the fiery rhetorical style of the period as based on the preconceived picture of «a raging, ferocious, uncool, demoralized black boy banging on the immaculate door of White Society, begging, not so much for political justice as for his own identity, and in the process consuming himself, so that in the final analysis, his destiny is at the mercy of the White Man.»[26]

To such indictments of protest on psychological and moral grounds was added the disillusionment caused by Euro-American neo-colonialism and the white backlash on the home front. Implicit in the genre had always been the assumption that the white world has a conscience, however dormant or torpid, to which it is possible to appeal. Protest literature had further assumed that the ideals and principles upon which the nation is built are sound and that, therefore, integration of black America into the mainstream culture is a desirable goal. Consequently, the protest writer had conceived of himself as an advocate of his people's rights and as an ambassador for their history and culture vis-à-vis whites in order to prove them worthy of admission. He had even at times felt called upon to act as the defender of American ideals and human rights when whites appeared to be corrupting them. In the second half of the decade, this traditional basis of protest writing foundered as the old trust yielded to a sense of the white world's malignancy, reflected in the widespread use of a rhetoric representing America as the «Fourth Reich,» guilty of «genocide» and of seeking a «final solution» to the race problem, policed by «fascist» state troopers,» and disposing of its dissenters by putting them in penitentiaries referred to as «concentration camps» and «gas chambers.» A more appropriate spelling, it was suggested, would be «Amerika.» To such a view, the old protest tradition could only be worse than useless, failing as it had always done to take account of the fundamental facts of white moral evasion and racist use of power.

This, then, was the new climate of thought and feeling for which the sensibility of anger sought to shape proper modes of expression, a vision of a world of malevolent aggression directed against the black race and threatening the survival of humanist ideals. What was felt to be required was a literature stripped of the illusory old idealisms and hopes for an egalitarian and color-blind society in the New World, a literature in which anger would not mean frustration, bitterness, and pleading, but a heroic and affirmative wrath. In a world in which the prime issues are survival and liberation, the literary artist must rise with the rest of the oppressed nation to seize control and power. Literary creation is verbal warfare and part of the revolutionary battle against the colonist now being waged for the minds of black people in preparation for the coming Armageddon. The new literature of anger was not to be written out of frustration and wailing, nor was its purpose to be apology. It was to be a literature devoted to demysti-

fying white power and simultaneously created out of a newfound
personal and collective black power. Informed by a new cynicism,
angry black writers in the 1960s started from a vision of ruthless
antiblack forces at work in their American and Western environment, but also from a breathtaking sense of being in league with
the rising, post-Western civilizations.

Turning away from his traditional white liberal audience, the
black writer increasingly addressed his own racial community,
joining in its struggle to survive and renovate itself socially and
morally. Deflected from its previous outlet in protest art, anger
fashioned new uses for itself in artistic modes and stances expressed in Third World imagery. Frequently, the racial writer was
defined as a freedom fighter or artist-warrior whose creative la-
bors are «survival motions» and acts of anticolonial liberation.
Works of art would be metaphorically described as «daggers,»
«bullets,» «fists,» «teeth,» or potent «poisons,» operating directly
and concretely in the world to destroy the hold of the oppressor on
the black mind. This strategy went far beyond the efforts of preceding generations to control the racial iconography by creating, in
the words written by James Weldon Johnson in 1922, «symbols
from within.»[27] The concern of the post-1965 generation was «the
deliberate desecration and smashing of idols, the turning inside out
of symbols, to which black writers are now proceeding with a
vengeance.»[28] An an example of this kind of ritual killing or
«desecration» of the oppressor's cultural images is Carolyne G.
Gerald's poem, a savage defamation and literary lynching of the
cherished mythical figure of the muse.[29]

A dramatization of the militant black nationalism of Malcolm
X, Baraka, and Fanon, the poem dissociates itself openly and self-
consciously from the «highbrow» stance of the white tradition:
poetry as precious and private «musing.» Its spirit and technique
are those of agitprop art: the use of plosives and hissing fricatives;
open vowels and diphthongs imitating shouting; diction and gram-
mar (verb-based, imperatives); ideographic exploitation of the
page to indicate the twists and turns of the erupting fury. Basically
dramatic in conception, the poem establishes a public situation in
which a collective act is staged in the form of a punitive ritual burning. A thundering voice is heard addressing an Afro-American
audience in a spirit of identification and solidarity(«we»):

> Dress the muse in black . . .
> No!
> Kill her!

Opening on a note of self-correction (to «dress the muse in black» would be simply to continue to ape the white convention of poetry as musing), the black preacherlike voice proceeds to hurl imprecations at the Caucasian goddess, variously called «Phony 'fay» and white «devil,» in a language that sounds like an inversion of evangelistic exhortation. The ritual burning has overtones of the purgative idol smashing of Fanon's colonial, an identity-creating act of profound significance. The deed done, the audience is called away in search of a new divinity of the arts in a world restored to its prewhite and prelapsarian innocence («The universe is black again.»). The dethroned muse will be succeeded by «our own saint,» suggesting a new conception of poetic expression fusing art, life, and the racial culture in stark contrast to the exclusive aestheticism of the European tradition.

Gerald's poem is an example of how the literary battle might be fought against the colonial master's power as exercised through his control of the language. The special province of anger within the greater war waged by the race should no longer be apology or pleading, but confrontation and attack in order to appropriate the linguistic medium, demystify the white enemy, diagnose the damage done to the black race in America, educate, and exhort.

A cleansing of the language was felt to be imperative to enable the artist to regenerate the racial group. A soldier in the war against the colonial controllers of language, engaged in the service of his race and the Afro-American nation, the black writer was now to channel his rage into other outlets than the traditional novels and poems of moral outcry. A new combative image, drawn from Third World national liberation struggles, increasingly replaced that of the «Negro» protest artist. In this new image there was no room for the traditional social moralism. In a white world felt to be without conscience, its spirit must be martial and its expression military.

Similarly, the celebrative pattern responded to the pressures of the times. Previous eulogies in literature of the Negro's heritage had usually been motivated by a desire to affirm his ultimate

Americanness. Even as Toomer, for example, erected his racial mythos in *Cane,* he viewed it in the context of America's passage from a rural to an urban order. The Southern Negro's culture is related to the quintessentially rural that alone has saving power in a modern American wasteland. Adopted for literary use by Baldwin and Ellison a generation later, the Negro's Negroness was invested with a meta-racial redemptive meaning in contemporary America. Their two symbolic figures — the black stranger in the Euro-American village and the invisible underground man in the big American city — appear as magnified Americans and exaggerated moderns whose role in our age is a priestly one. A similar notion persisted in the early thought of Amiri Baraka. After paying tribute to surviving Africanisms in religion, music, and folklore in «Myth of a 'Negro Literature'» (1962),[30] he proceeded to define the distinctive features of Negro culture in much the same terms as the preceding generation, that is, as a heightened version of the American experience. The Negro is the archetypal American, his experience is «evidence of a more profound America» whose accumulated black wisdom and long stewardship in suffering are assigned redemptive value. To celebrate this black and American wisdom is, properly speaking, the business of Negro art.

As the 1960s progressed, however, Baraka's generation underwent the conversion to «Blackness» that altered the basis for artistic celebration of the racial heritage. For the «more profound America» were substituted the concept of an autonomous Afro-American nation and an exclusive diasporic and anti-Western identity. Whereas to preceding generations, the Negro's «double consciousness» had been his unique resource, to Baraka's young contemporaries it became the primary symptom of his malady. In their writings, derogatory references to Du Bois's idea were frequent, even as they embraced him and included him in their pantheon of heroes. Instead was projected the ideal of a unified non-Western sensibility, merging ideas of a distinctive and peculiar racial *Geist,* a separate culture, and a Black Nation.

Music and its lexicon were of great importance in redefining and expressing the celebrative impulse in the new Afro-American writing. Negatively, this was done by opposing the symphony and the symphony orchestra to jazz and the jazz band in order to con-

vey the sense of two incompatible cultures and the aesthetic modes
derived from them. Turned into symbolic microcosms, symphonic
music and the manner of its performance became mirrors of the
antihumanism of Western art and the destructive intellectual and
social values sustaining it. In an essay characteristic of the period,
Ortiz M. Walton[31] equated the symphony orchestra with three
other and analogous products of Western societies: the industrial
plant, the machine, and political autocracy. The invention of the
symphony orchestra is perceived as an event symbolizing «the
complete rationalization of music,» including attendant developments of specialization, rigid divisions and hierarchies. Its functioning is structurally parallel to «an assembly-line operation . . . organized along lines of maximal efficiency,» making no allowance
for individual deviations or audience participation, and rigidly
controlled by a «foreman or conductor» whose technical know-
how secures «the normal functioning of the machine.» Its underlying principle is an ideal of perfect rational order, a static structure fixed through notation, and rehearsed mechanically. At base
it is a totalitarian system: «The symphony . . . is a dictatorship.
There is a rigidity of form and craft practice — a virtual enslave-
ment of the individual to the autocratic conductor.» Thus the
proudest product of Western musical achievement was turned into
a symbolic reflection of a repressive and antihumanistic aesthetic.

   The principles of aesthetic creation pitted against this conception of art were those of black music, seen as African survivals
largely untouched by the hegemony of the slave master's culture.
Those elements of the African heritage that did not have artifacts
as their end products, that is, religion, dance, and music, eluded
white control and remained in many respects intact. Hence black
musical expression is of a different order and inherently at odds
with the Western tradition. Rooted in a sensibility whose
apprehension of reality is based on an understanding of time as
perpetual flow, Afro-American music is fundamentally
«improvisational» and «non-matrixed.» In order to be faithful to
its innermost nature, this music must, like all black art, conceive
of itself as movement: «Art goes. Art is not fixed. Art can not be
fixed. Art is change, like music, poetry, and writing are, when conceived.»[32] Refusing to move against time or to arrest and fix reality
in static structures, it fearlessly embraces flux and motion. Per-

ceiving fluctuation not as chaos, but as the creative principle of the universe, it is not concerned to impose order or system. Increasingly, black American music came to be viewed as the embodiment of a nonwhite, non-Western «continuous repository of black consciousness,»[33] closely related to an ethic of action and immediacy with a high valuation on affective behavior, a collective art, geared to communal experience and celebrative affirmation of the racial group.

The musician no longer held the same meaning as for Ellison, Baldwin, and even the early Kelley. To them he had been under his black skin an archhuman or archmodern whose priestly office is to exorcise chaos and bring to light the common humanity of all men. The new vision of him was as «the reemerging African»[34] in black American culture, a vatic figure whose performances are ritual ceremonials of the Afro-American nation. He is a pioneer in the expression of true black sensibility, creating and recreating in his art his own and his people's *négritude*. The artistic process in which he is involved is analogous to the African custom of building temples and statues of mud, that are washed away by the rains and then rebuilt. Similarly the music of Afro-America is a perishable art, traditionally preserved and communicated through perpetual creation and recreation.

The importance of this musical tradition as model and exemplar for black celebrative self-expression in literature is hard to overestimate. Its relationship to both the verbal and the visual arts was seen as symbiotic, the same freely expressive styles operating in Afro-American writing, painting, and music alike. Thus to the poet Lance Jeffers the interchangeability of «pen» and «horn»[35] was as natural as was the African-American literary-musical analogy to Ishmael Reed in the creative life of his writer-hero Quickskill: his «writing was his Hoodoo . . . his typewriter was his drum he danced to.»[36]

The impact of this African-American musical aesthetic on the young literary celebrants may be specifically observed in the tendency to view the poem, fiction, or play as analogous to the nonmatrixed, swinging movements of jazz, the sophisticated «scream» of the native African, the field holler of the black American slave, and the soul shouts of James Brown. It further underlies the frequent metaphorical representation of black litera-

ry works as force, energy, «solar concerts,» or «black radiance,»
as these works embody heroic black lives or the Black Nation as
actually existing or as conceived at a later, more fully realized
stage. Finally, it is reflected in the tendency to remove all hierar-
chical distinctions between art and life, and between artist, work,
and audience.

The literary rhetoric of the sixties abounds in semimystical
statements of black people *being* the poets and the audience as well
as the poems. The writer-singer of black beauty merges with the
song and the racial audience in a totality of expression that parta-
kes of the nature of litanies and incantations in the celebration of
black American and Pan-African peoplehood and *force vitale*. No
longer an affirmer of the Negro's Americanness, the black literary
artist is the celebrator of a unique racial genius, offering in his
work heightened glimpses of the black *Geist* fulfilled. He serves his
people, guarding and preserving its historical memory. He is the
miracle worker, the creator of symbols and the singer of heroes,
«working his juju with the word on the world.»[37] In this way,
while continuing the celebrative mode, black writers in the 1960s
radically transformed its meaning and purpose. In singing the
praise of Afro-American nationhood and the primordial emoti-
veness of black people, they sought to join in the adventure of
shaping a post-American and post-Western humanism that they
saw being born into the world in our time.

Thus the strands come together in the design of the new black
writing. Whether their art were wrath-filled ritual destructions of
«the white thing» or joyful homages to *soul* and peoplehood,
black writers saw themselves as being about the historical task of
de-Westernizing their culture in preparation for a new era of
«afterwhiteness color.»[38] Toward this end black literary creativity
must be directed and made functional. Whether as «desecrators»
or «necromancers,» they responded to a shared awareness of
living in new patterns of history. In the endeavor to express that
awareness in terms drawn from their New World experience, they
found the deepest meaning of their art.

Notes

[1] Samuel W. Allen, «Negritude and Its Relevance to the American Negro Writer,» in *Cavalcade,* ed. Arthur P. Davis and Saunders Redding (Boston: Houghton Mifflin Co., 1971), p. 618. Allen's essay was initially written in 1958-59 and presented as a paper at the First Conference of Negro Writers in 1959.

[2] *Ibid., p. 618.*

[3] Arthur P. Davis, «Integration and Race Literature,» *Phylon, 17* (1956): 141-46, and John Lash, «The Conditioning of Servitude: A Critical Summary of Literature by and about Negroes in 1957,» *Phylon, 19* (1958): 143-53.

[4] Ralph Ellison, «Remarks at The American Academy of Arts and Sciences Conferences on the Negro American, 1965,» *New Black Voices,* ed. Abraham Chapman (New York: New American Library, 1972), p. 404. Though Ellison's remarks date from 1965, one may safely assume that it represents his view in the late fifties. His view of the essential Americanness of black American culture has remained a constant throughout his career.

[5] Blyden Jackson, «A Golden Mean for the Negro Novel,» *CLA Journal, 3* (1959): p. 87.

[6] Philip Butcher, «The Younger Novelists and the Urban Negro,» *CLA Journal, 4* (1961): p. 196.

[7] Arna Bontemps, «The New Black Renaissance,» *Negro Digest, 13* (1961): 52-58.

[8] James Baldwin, «Letters from a Journey,» *Black Voices,* ed. Herbert Hill (London: Elek Books, 1964), pp. 42, 47.

[9] Reprinted in Cruse's collection of essays *Rebellion or Revolution* (New York: William Morrow & Co., 1968).

[10] Entitled «Negro Writing in America.»

[11] Baldwin, «Autobiographical Notes,» *Notes of a Native Son* (New York: Bantam Books, 1964), p. 4.

[12] «The Problems of the Negro Writer,» in *Black and White in American Culture,* ed. Jules Chametzky and Sidney Kaplan (New York: Viking Press, 1969), pp. 360-61. Originally published in *The Massachusetts Review, 6* (1964-65).

[13] *Ibid,* p. 363.

[14] Allan, «Negritude and its Relevance,» p. 625.

[15] Langston Hughes, ed., *An African Treasury* (New York: Pyramid Books, 1961), *Freedomways, 2* no. 4 (1962).

[16] Harold Isaacs, «The American Negro and Africa: Some Notes,» *Phylon, 20* (1959): p. 220.

[17] The following quotations are from Clarke's «The New Afro-American Nationalism,» *Freedomways, 1* (1961): 285-95, and Cruse's «Negro Nationalism's New Wave,» collected in *Rebellion or Revolution* (originally published 1962).

[18] Clarence Major, ed., *The New Black Poetry* (New York: International Publishers, 1969).

[19] Mercer Cook and Stephen E. Henderson, *The Black Militant Writer in Africa and the United States* (Madison: University of Wisconsin Press, 1969), p. 67.

[20] Sonia Sanchez, ed., *We Be Word Sorcerers* (New York: Bantam, 1973).

[21] Nikki Giovanni, *Gemini* (New York: The Viking Press, 1971), p. 34.

[22] Cook and Henderson, *The Black Militant Writer in Africa and the United States,* p. 118.

[23] Eugene Redmond, *Drumvoices: The Mission of Afro-American Poetry* (Garden City N.Y.): Doubleday, 1976, Chap. 6.

[24] Cook and Henderson, *The Black Militant Writer in Africa and the United States,* p. 118.

[25] In *The Black Aesthetic,* ed. Addison Gayle, Jr. (New York: Doubleday & Co.), pp. 327-48.

[26] Cited by Fuller, *ibid.,* p. 346.

[27] James Weldon Johnson, ed., *The Book of American Negro Poetry* (New York: Harcourt, Brace & World, 1922), p. 41.

[28] Carolyne G. Gerald, «The Black Writer and His Role,» *The Black Aesthetic,* pp. 354-55. (Originally published 1969.)

[29] *Ibid.,* pp., 355-56.

[30] *Home* (New York: William Morrow & Co., 1966).

[31] Ortiz M. Walton, «A Comparative Analysis of the African and the Western Aesthetics,» *The Black Aesthetic,* pp. 154-64. All quotations from this essay.

[32] James T. Stewart, «The Development of the Black Revolutionary Artist,» *Black Fire,* ed. LeRoi Jones and Larry Neal (New York: William Morrow & Co., 1968), pp. 4-5.

[33] Ron Wellburn, «The Black Aesthetic Imperative,» *The Black Aesthetic,* p. 126.

[34] Kimberly W. Benston, *The Renegade and the Mask* (New Haven and London: Yale Univ. Press, 1976), p. 89.

[35] Lance Jeffers, «Afroamerican Literature: The Conscience of Man,» in *New Black Voices,* ed. Abraham Chapman (1971, reprint ed. New York and Toronto: New American Library, 1972), p. 506.

[36] Ishmael Reed, *Flight to Canada* (New York: Random House, 1976), p. 89.

[37] Larry Neal, «And Shine Swam On,» *Black Fire,* p. 655.

[38] Amiri Baraka, *RAISE RACE RAYS RAZE* (1967, reprint ed., New York: Random House, 1972), p. 34.

3

The «Negro-to-Black Conversion» in Contemporary Afro-American Autobiography: Two Patterns

The centrality of autobiography in the tradition of black American literary expression is by now a historical and critical commonplace. Since its inception in the memoirs of fugitive slaves in the mid-nineteenth century (though the first recorded example of the genre is *A Narrative of the Uncommon sufferings and Surprising Deliverance of Briton Hammon, a Negro Man,* published in Boston in 1760), black autobiography has evolved into a highly self-conscious medium, used by the races's literary craftsmen for a variety of purposes, personal as well as public, polemical, and propagandistic. Including among its numbers an unusually high proportion of classic works, such as Frederick Douglass's *Narrative* (1845, later expanded), Booker T. Washington's *Up From Slavery* (1902), parts of W. E. B. Du Bois's *Souls of Black Folk* (1903), Richard Wright's *Black Boy* (1945), and *The Autobiography of Malcolm X* (1965), black autobiography might fairly claim to occupy the literary and cultural position of a racial epic. It is perhaps in this body of «mythicized» personal narratives of bondage and freedom, of trial and overcoming, and of visions of new worlds that the Afro-American writer touches the epic tradition most directly.

This collective and generalized quality persists in the extraordinary outpouring of autobiographical writing that distinguished the decade of the 1960s. Written with few exceptions by the generation born after the Second World War and whose formative period coincided with the turbulent years of the civil rights movement and black nationalism, these works tend to subordinate the individual to the representative and to project personal stories as moral parables. Nowhere is this convention more clearly seen than in the treatment of that distinctive and archetypal motif in the new autobiographical literature: the «Negro-to-Black Conversion.» Submerging the private in the group experience, these stories typically cast their authors' personae as model selves and public exemplars. Furthermore, ironically modifying the classic rhetorical posture of the mature, definitive, and complete self reviewing his previous life, these young and committed autobiographers adopt a stance of a constantly evolving perspective in which the shedding of «Negroness» is followed by initiation into a «Blackness» whose very nature is a dynamic and creative flux.

The «Negro-to-Black Conversion» as a distinctive and recognizable psychological phenomenon of the 1960s has been subjected to professional analysis by William E. Cross, jr.[1] Defining change in self-perception and behavior, Cross delimits five stages: «pre-encounter (pre-discovery) stage;»«encounter (discovery) stage;» «immersion-emersion stage;» «internalization stage;» and finally the «commitment stage». In the first stage, the black person is «programmed to view and think of the world as being non-Black, anti-Black, or the opposite of Black,» that is to say, his «world-view is determined by Euro-American determinants.» Such preencounter persons prefer to be called «Negro,» «civilized,» «colored,» «human being,» or «American citizen.»

In the second stage, he is exposed to some catalytic event or encounter that triggers off a questioning of old assumptions and the beginning reinterpretation of his situation in the light of such concepts as «Black History,» «Black Power,» or «Black is beautiful.»

The third stage is characterized by full immersion in and often idealization of everything «Black,» accompanied by a withdrawal from everything perceived as associated with the white world and, frequently, confrontations with «whitey.» The internalization stage is the most difficult, and some fail to pass beyond it, falling into a nihilistic position of total rejection as their high expectations are not fulfilled, or they fixate in a third-stage hatred of white people after painful confrontations. Those who pass successfully through this stage are able to «internalize and incorporate aspects of the immersion-emersion experience into their self-concept,» achieving a feeling of inner security and psychological liberation.

The final stage involves the actualization and «living» of the newly acquired identity and commitment to a plan of action, accompanied by a relaxation or more realistic containment of the hatred of whites.

What Cross stated in the vocabulary of psychology and the social sciences, literary intellectuals set forth more loosely in terms of
a crisis of consciousness and creative sensibility. For black writers,
too, «Negroness» and «Blackness» were important categories
whose ideological implications might differ, but whose essential
reality could not be doubted. In autobiographical writing particularly, the conversion experience, whether assumed or actually
dramatized in the narrative, is a central presence reflecting the
intellectual and moral upheaval that so often led to a repudiation
of the traditional Euro-American anchorage in favor of a post-
occidental cultural identification. This is the design that emerges
from the diversity of personal stories by Malcolm X, Eldridge
Cleaver, Leslie Alexander Lacy, Amiri Baraka, George Jackson,
Julius Lester, Bobby Seale, Huey Newton, H. Rap Brown, Addison Gayle, Jr., Angela Davis, Nikki Giovanni, Anne Moody and,
in her own way, Maya Angelou.

What deserves further notice is the readiness with which this
conversion theme fits into the larger pattern of rage and celebration that permeates Afro-American literary expression in the
1960s.

Interestingly, these two stances are contained in the interview
material on which Cross's study is based, though the author
makes no attempt to place them in such a context:

> Yea, it all started when they shot Brother King. Honkies
> planned that shit and it really shook me up so bad until I be-
> gan to see what was really happening to Black people. For
> awhile I could no longer stand to be around white people. I
> hated all their guts and on some days I swear I wanted to kill
> the first honky I saw. You know what, I even began to feel
> that we were better than they were because we had so much
> soul and love. . . .

> To walk around 125 and Lenox Avenue is a powerful thing,
> can you dig it? When I see so many beautiful Black folks try-
> ing to make it, doing everything just to stay alive, yet still
> being able to sing and dance in such a soulful manner, it just
> blows my mind and I sometimes want to cry tears of joy. Can
> you dig it? I'm part of it all! I see Black, feel Black, oh how
> wonderful it is to be Black.

These accounts suggest a distinction that coincides rather closely with the traditional dual pattern. The experience recorded in the first statement sets off from what is perceived as a racist and conspiratorial antiblack act, producing an almost uncontrollable rage that toward the end is gradually converted into a defiant sense of moral superiority and repudiation of white norms. The second moves from an epiphanic moment of discovery in an all-black street crowd of a soulful and heroic ethos to joyful abandon and assertion of its beauty.

It is this dual pattern of experience that the best Afro-American authobiographical writing of the 1960s raises to the level of art. Frequently both elements in the duality are operative within the same conversion experience to the point of making any separation of them schematic and arbitrary. Any discussion of, for example, *The Autobiography of Malcolm X* must take account of both aspects, the persona's fiery wrath at the discovery of the white man's plundering of black history no less than his joy at the breathtaking spectacle of black political and cultural power during his African pilgrimage. Inextricably interwoven, the two responses exist as constituent parts within the totality of his «Negro-to-Black» transformation.

Essentially, however, Malcolm's treatment of this material is at best semiliterary. The great significance of his narrative to formal black autobiography lies in its making the dual folk experience of rage and celebration visible and available for self-conscious aesthetic presentation. Thus the perspective in which it should be viewed is as an intermediate stage between the folk experience recorded and analyzed by Cross and the literary form given to it by black literary autobiographers.

The semiliterary nature of the story is obvious from Alex Haley's account of the mode of its production no less than from its reception. Malcolm came out of an oral culture that, like all nonliterate cultures, is functional, direct, and performance-oriented. As recorded by his ghostwriter, the telling of the story took the form of dramatic events:

> Then it was during recalling the early Harlem days that Malcolm X really got carried away. One night, suddenly, wildly, he jumped up from his chair and, incredibly, the fear-

some black demagogue was scat-singing and popping his fin-
gers, «re-bop-de-bop-blap-blam-» and then grabbing a verti-
cal pipe with one hand (as the girl partner) he went jubilantly
lindy-hopping around, his coattail and the long legs and the
big feet flying as they had in those Harlem days. And then almost as suddenly, Malcolm X caught himself and sat down,
and for the rest of the session he was decidedly grumpy.
(Epilogue to the Grove Press edition, p. 391.)

Similarly, the popular success of his story rested not on literary
qualities but on its projection of a heroic black masculinity revealing itself in the acts of a doer and prime mover in close touch with
the racial culture. In itself only marginally «literary» in creative
origin and appeal, Malcolm's book helped lift the dual folk
experience of his time from spontaneity into consciousness, from
shapelessness into narrative-dramatic form.

Against this background, it is of interest to examine examples of
a mature literary presentation in autobiography of the two
patterns of rage and celebration. Two recent autobiographical
works lend themselves admirably to this purpose. What makes
them particularly useful is the fact that while most stories tend to
blend the two strands, these two isolate them in almost pure form,
offering us a rare opportunity to study directly the specific dyna-
mics of each. In «The Son of My Father» and «The Heretics»[2]
Gayle and Baraka project selves in crisis whose inner conversion
dramas are externalized in narratives plotted as rites of passage
within the dual framework of rage and celebration. A fall from
«Negroness» is followed by a restoration to a primordial «Blackness» linking the self with the progressive and upward historical
surge of non-Western cultures. The mediating experiences in the
two initiations are, on the one hand, the releasing of passionate
anger by racial humiliation and, on the other, the epiphanic discovery of an extant and intact substratum of vital black folk life.
Together they offer conveniently encapsulated illustrations of the
dual structure of one of the most distinctive black experiences in
the 1960s.

The superior piece in Gayle's volume is «The Son of My
Father,» which, though it should be read both against the background of the other personal essays in the book and his full-length

autobiography, *Wayward Child* (1977), offers a self-contained statement of the contemporary sensibility of black rage. The particulars of the story involve two ugly acts of discrimination followed by an emotional breakdown, education in white schools, association with white liberals and the experience of being a token Negro, an interracial love affair, and the embracing of a militant black nationalism. Through an extensive texture of allusion, imagery, and irony, the narrative magnifies the experience of an individual and historical self into a collective and «mythic» story of the shedding of «Negroness» and the painstaking reconstituting of a truly «Black» identity. The heightening devices range from literary allusion (Dante, Goethe, Shelley, Keats, Kafka, Dostoyevski, Shakespeare, Plato, Emerson), historical reference (the Middle Passage, slavery, the Great Migration), religion (Christianity and Oriental religions), and mythology (the Narcissus myth), ironies, and symbolic imagery (fire, water, blood, boxing) to calculated typecasting. In this way, locale and narrative incidents as well as character and authorial comments are heightened. The story is cast in epic terms as an «odyssey,» beginning «early on a Monday morning, on a dismal, overcast day in May,» and acting itself out in a Kafkaesque world of menacing mystery. It is a world inhabited by characters hovering on the edge of allegory: the «cracker» storeowner, the guilt-ridden restaurant manager, the covertly racist liberal intellectuals, the employment agency transformed into a combined latter-day plantation and slave market complete with white master, field hands (the older black men), and houseslave (the light-complexioned assistant, «a charming, brownskinned girl of about twenty-one, heavily rouged, her hair in pompadour, her false eyelashes flickering as in amusement»).

The autobiographical persona himself is made representative through association with the racial exodus from the South and with parents typefying historical patterns of «Negroness.» The controlling archetypal metaphors are those of desecration of the parent figure and the night journey, or descent into Hell, which at its lowest point miraculously turns into a cleansing «baptism in my own tears,» the tears giving birth to a «fire» of hatred and vengeful feelings through which is cast out the demon of «Negroness.» The last stage is the solemn, almost ritualistic «dedication» to the fearful truths of being black in a white world through utter rejection of its ethical norms, providing a basis for the salvaging and restoring of an unadulterated «Black» self, that though continuing to live in the West, is no longer of it.

The persona's initial «Negro» identity includes various aspects. Gayle portrays him as suspended between two traditional modes of «Negroness»: his mother's Protestant Christianity and his father's Marxist communism, both of which involve self-definition on the white man's terms. Other aspects of this false identity are his victimization by white definitions of him in terms of racist stereotypes, as «an accursed son of Ham» in the South and as a «noble savage» in the North, and his being the target of the two historical methods of black oppression: physical violence («the rope around your neck» in the Virginia he has fled from), and, in Ellison's term,[3] the «lobotomy» of Northern liberal rhetoric. He admits to having internalized the values and standards of white America and, in consequence, to having suffered a loss of self-knowledge that has forced him into submissive behavior, dissimulation, and self-eroding role playing. Imposed from without, this corrupt «Negroness» is symbolically summed up in the portering job he has held. In the past he has been a creature laboring under the burden of the possessions of others.

This false self is discarded after his realization of the anti-humanistic nature of white civilization and the fundamental truth that the victim is always alone. Association with whites, even the «best» among them, significantly fails to restore in him the sense of self and dignity required to survive on his own terms. Only an act of radical repudiation of the whole ethical basis of Western culture and return to the racial community can achieve this aim.

This inner crisis and revolution of consciousness is formally worked out, it would seem, in terms of a process of reversing or ironically transforming two Euro-American moral and cultural traditions. The first is the story of Christ's Passion. In the final scene, the persona's imagination moves back in time to the Easter of the Crucifixion, identifying with the militantly nationalistic masses in the streets of Jerusalem in their angry shouts for Barrabas's freedom while mocking the «pitiable, feeble moan» of forgiveness coming from the cross. Christ appears as the greatest of all slave masters whose ethic of compassion, submission to injustice, and forgiveness of one's enemies must be rejected. For the contemporary sensibility of black rage, Christ's Passion as an expression of a moral ideal is a ludicrous hoax that must be demystified and shown in its true historical function of conferring legitimacy on Western racist oppression.

Standing the Passion narrative on its head and moving a marginal figure in the tradition to the center of the story, Gayle projects Barabbas, an Eastern revolutionary nationalist in Roman-Western captivity, as a worthy hero for an oppressed people. Traditionally seen by Christians as an exemplification of the effects of substitutionary atonement, Barabbas is transformed in the imagination of the persona into a model of self-assertive behavior in the face of oppression. Furthermore, associated historically with the party of the Zealots, he also suggests ideas of violent resistance, nationhood, and fidelity to the racial-ethnic heritage in a time of corrupting imperialist influence.

In his handling of the Western moral myth, Gayle has so engineered its elements as to subvert its traditional meaning in favor of an alternative model of personal and racial behavior. Through identification with Barabbas, Gayle's persona detaches the black man from two thousand years of Western moral thought, returning him to his pre-Western, pre-Christian origins.

The second instance of an ironically transformed traditional pattern is the persona's reversal of the traditional infantilization of the black man, as reflected in the Southern custom of addressing him as «boy» and in the condescending paternalism of Northern liberal rhetoric. Expressive of supremacist assumptions of black inferiority to be remedied only under white custodianship, these practices conceal what in reality amounts to a vicious castration of the black psyche through implantation of subservience and dependency on a white father image. The elimination of this syndrome in the newborn «Black» self of Gayle's persona is demonstrated through an inversion of the established pattern.

Now it is America that is shown in the role of a frightened and guilty child as her black people, reveling in the glory of their new-found «Blackness,» rise in rage to assert themselves: «America is at that desperate stage when, feeling the threat from her long-neglected citizenry, she needs some supporting, sustaining voice to assure her that the neglected are still, despite all, hopeful, passive, and restrained.» The creature that the white world has insisted on defining and treating as a primitive, a child, and a ward has now taken the matter of his life and death into his own hands, thereby coming of age. Having stepped out of the white American scheme, the new «Black» man is no longer bound by the categories and terms of that scheme. This makes of him a new creature, the member of a new species, the maker and namer of his own unique space within a new world morally and spiritually anchored outside the West.

Such, then, is the new self-concept of Gayle's autobiographical persona. Born in fiery rage, it has risen Phoenix-like from the ashes of «Negroness,» a new self that for all its continuity with the past appears almost like a mutant: a post-Christian and post-Western black man, the harbinger of a new humanity:

> I am, I know, a desperate man, a cynical man and, perhaps, according to Freudian psychology which can in no way explain me, a sick man. Some of my friends would add, quickly, a mad man. I do not object. Perhaps to be sane in this society is the best evidence of insanity. To repress all that I know, to keep hidden in my subconscious all that I feel may inevitably force me to those acts of desperation which I am capable of viewing here, frankly and honestly with a certain objective detachment.

Projected not as a fixed and final entity, it is a self *in extremis,* endowed with a peculiar, «mad» lucidity and poised on the edge of revolutionary action. Flaunting his contempt of the efforts of Western science to explain and contain him, he also accepts honestly and without a trace of guilt his antiwhite feelings. Lucidly and in full consciousness he hates, channeling his rage so as to give it a purgative effect in ridding him of the last vestiges of whiteness and «Negroness.»

Compared with the experience of the preceding generation, the experience of Gayle's persona suggests the distance traveled by many black writers in the 1960s. While sharing with Ellison's unnamed narrator his insistence on being recognized as an individual, the self of «Son of My Father» is defined in new terms. Where the former, having shed his various false roles, could only reaffirm the cardinal American virtues and ideals his grandfather had believed in, the moral revolution of the latter has necessitated a «killing» of his ancestry and exclusive commitment to a morality of an eye for an eye and a politics of racial unity and antiwhite confrontation.

Similar differences distinguish «Son of My Father» from Baldwin's autobiographical essays «Notes of a Native Son» and «Stranger in the Village.» The hero of the first of these is moved by a compelling urge to reconcile himself with the legacy imposed on him by his father and to incorporate it in his new life. At the same time, the black «stranger» in the European «village» seeks to convert his strangeness into a resource with the power to redeem the West. Sonship and being a stranger are also basic conditions in the fate of Gayle's persona. But for the latter there can be no reconciliation with the father's «Negro» heritage and his strangeness has meaning only as a separate and unique «Blackness» to be pursued in withdrawal from a moribund Western Culture.

The System of Dante's Hell contains an equally mythicized account of a *rite de passage* that, though different, follows an ultimately convergent route from «Negroness» to «Blackness.» For our purpose, it will be sufficient to examine the final chapter («The Heretics»), which is organized around the actual conversion, and which, through retrospective reference, offers a condensed representation of the whole «foetal drama» of the birth of a new self. The fact of its separate publication in *New American Story* is also indicative of its structural autonomy.

On the ratio of fact and fiction in the narrative, Baraka himself has offered the following comment: «Much of it is autobiography — from situations I have been in, but most of it is projections of ideas, much later. . . . They germinate in experience. . . . Most of the time I move from real people that I know, or I move from real experiences.»[4] Baraka's comment suggests that to an even greater extent than Gayle's, the speaking I in *System,* while firmly rooted in actuality, is a carefully constructed persona investing the private story with public significance. In the narrative itself, the generalizing effect is achieved through the use of myth, archetype, and literary allusion. Thus the adventures of the black protagonist are patterned on the archetypal descent into Hell, specifically on the model of the ninth circle of Dante's Inferno. Another such fusion is the simultaneous casting of the hero as a quester for the Holy

Grail of «Blackness,» the lost Prodigal, Odysseus, and Dantean arch-heretic. Within this overall framework, to which may be added quest patterns related to a mother figure and home, more localized patterns are at work: his resemblance to «a dead soul from Charon's bark» as he steps off the bus for his encounter with his forgotten roots; the projection of his self-condemnation after the initiation as «the ultimate Narcissus gesture,» characteristic of all identity quests; the description of the dream setting of the final struggle for selfhood as an archetypal purgatorial «cave»; and finally, as pointed out by Kimberly Benston, the implied Orphic analogy in the representation of the struggle of the resurrected black self to remain faithful to the racial heritage revealed to him as he returns to the world:

> In this last exorcistic ritual, Baraka's Orphic being is subjected to the mythic *sparmagós,* or disemberment, upon its emergence from Hell. He is fractured yet he is one, and through his ordeal he guarantees the possibility of later assuming the Orphic role of shaman, the singer-prophet capable of establishing harmony and unity out of the shattered fragments of black civilization. The descent to the Bottom is not, finally, a descent to hell but a triumphant return to life.[5]

However, myth and archetype are not the only routes to representativeness for Baraka's persona. Military imagery serves the same function. The abbreviation «awol,» as applied to the black protagonist, takes on a double significance. First, the literal expression — «a wolf on the loose» — suggests his initial dehumanized state as a «Negro» or imitation white. Secondly, its technical meaning of «absent without leave» becomes suggestively ironic when used as a description of the relationship of his quest to the white world: the black identity quest must be undertaken without the permission or assistance of whites. In fact, the Air Force base itself assumes symbolic overtones. Located in the Louisiana backwoods, the heart of Southern «crackerdom,» it is not merely the «whitest» of the armed services. It is also the most mechanized, offering an expressive metaphor of the black man's situation in a Western world of racism, technology, and power. It is within such a context that his quest for «Blackness» is undertaken as an unauthorized and «illegal» act.

Appropriately, the formal framework set up for the «Negro-to-Black» conversion of Baraka's persona also derives from non-white and non-Western sources. As the black Prodigal, «unfocussed on blackness,» moves toward discovery and acceptance of his true self, the reader is brought to an awareness of the language of the story operating in a manner analogous to jazz. Jerome Klinkowitz has pointed out the general influence of Baraka's musical studies on his fiction and, with specific reference to *System,* the structuring of Dante's nine circles as «an imitation of musical improvisations» working through «sensually cumulative successions of tones, moods, and colors.»[6] This accords with the shift one observes in Baraka's attitude to language away from words as semantic units and means of rational discourse and communication toward a use of language that will charge words with the immediacy of jazz sounds and rhythms. Hence the absence of transitional passages, the frequent disruptions in the narrative flow, and the constant presence and movement of images (moon, blood, night, water).

Without denying the influence of fictional modernism or Beat theories of spontaneous writing, it is important to realize Baraka's «racialization» of his prose medium through analogy with black music as the self embraces «Blackness.» Similarly the use of Dante is not an imitation of a Western literary model. *The Divine Comedy* also derives from Arabic narrative traditions, and part of its function in his fictionalized autobiography is to provide his story with a non-Western genealogy.

Within this generalized framework, a sequence of scenes is placed, beginning with the arrival in the black section of Shreveport of the persona and his friend on an illegal leave from the nearby Air Force base, soon to be followed by his encounter with a black female Vergil, Peaches, who guides him into the mysteries of the life-style and ethos of the unassimilated black folk of the ghetto. After attempting to escape this underworld, he is beaten senseless by a gang of black thugs — a punitive action brought against the «Negro» renegade, reminiscent of similar actions in Baraka's plays. In a dream scene, his final, though precariously defended, redemption is secured.

The movement of the autobiographical persona from «Negroness» to «Blackness» is different from, but complementary to, that of Gayle's. The tone in which his initial state is described is overtly satirical. The two black «wolves on the loose» are «imitation white boys» whose «head(s) (are) out to lunch.» Their inner lives are a «cardboard moonless world.» The ridiculing of «Negroness» continues with intimations of psychopathology, disease, chaos, and death in the persona's awareness of the «dead maelstrom of my head, a sickness,» persisting even after his initiation as «an ugliness (sitting) inside me waiting.» The diagnosis implied in this imagery emphasizes two particularly damaging syndromes: the near-schizoid schism between body, emotion, and mind, and a paralyzing solipsism. The first is symbolized by his internalization of the values of a white academic literary education («Thomas, Joyce, Eliot, Pound») that has caused his personality to be «(s)plit open down the center, which is the early legacy of the black man unfocussed on blackness.» The dichotomy of what is seen and taught and desired opposed to what is felt.» Although attracted by the elegance of the Euro-American literary masters, he comes to realize that this attraction functions as a decadent verbal titillation alienating him from his noncerebral faculties and from his own people living and suffering in the world. Eventually he finds himself «locked in a lightless shaft» of privacy and self-contemplating stupor. It is from this nadir that the self must rise in order to be regenerated.

The potential for rebirth is located both in the quester himself and in his environment. The moonlit Southern night with the silhouettes of sinister trees against the sky speaks of the horrors perpetrated against the black man, but the «crimson heavy blood of a race, concealed in those absolute nights,» the accumulated legacy of centuries of violence, also possesses the sacramental power to activate his slumbering racial memory, making him «(a)live to mystery» as he wanders between dewdrops having the «simple elegance of semen on the single buds of air.»

Descending to «The Bottom,» the all-black night spot that is to be the scene of birth of the embryonic black self and the star of its *ascesis,* he enters a world whose ethos is totally antithetical to that symbolized by the air base and the literary heroes of academia: a world of violent smell and color, of fast rapping and jiving, of bad-mouthing, signifying, and «the dozzens,» of blues rhythms and «soul» screams. Plunged into a dancing rite with Peaches, his

black female Vergil, he undergoes a complete transformation of
self, cutting the umbilical cord of Western culture and grafting
himself back on to the genealogical tree of the Mother Continent.

> The dancing like a rite no one knew, or had use for outside
> their secret lives. The flesh they felt when they moved, or I felt
> all their flesh and was happy and drunk and looked at the
> black faces knowing all the world that they were my own, and
> lusted at that anonymous America I broke out of, and long
> for it now, where I am.
>
> We danced, this face and I, close so I had her sweat in my
> mouth, her flesh the only sound my brain could use. Stinking,
> and the music over us like a sky, choked any other movement
> off. I danced. And my history was there, had passed no
> further. Where it ended, here, the light white talking jig, died
> in the arms of some sentry of Africa. Some short-haired witch
> out of my mother's most hideous dreams. I was nobody now,
> mama. Nobody. Another secret nigger. No one the white
> world wanted or would look at. (My mother shot herself. My
> father killed by a white tree fell on him. The sun, now,
> smothered. Dead.

Thus his imitation white self dies and a truly «Black» self is re-
born. The apotheosis of the persona has been effected through
exposure to and participation in the communal rituals of the racial
group, discovered in the same ancestral South to which Kelley returns in much of his work. The rest of «The Heretics» records the
attempts of the discarded «Negroness» to lure the resurrected
«Black» self away from its gains. It ends with a dream sequence
set in a «cavern,» apparently patterned on «threshing-floor» con-
versions in black churches, in which the hero, clinging to the old
self as symbolized by the book he is reading from, falls weeping on
the floor with black men and women dancing around the prostrate
sinner while they pour a sacramental libation of whisky on him.
The scene suggests the final, though precariously maintained,
triumph of «Blackness.»

Both Gayle and Baraka project black selves in crisis. Their
developments are different, but complementary. Having shed their
«Negroness,» they assume a new identity through rituals of baptis-

mal immersion in tears of anger or in a pristine black cultural matrix as found in a Southern black community untouched by Yankee free enterprise and European education. The resurrected selves are left, realistically, struggling to consolidate their dearly bought victories in the face of persistent efforts of the old «Negroness» to reassert itself. The «Blackness» of Gayle's persona is stated in terms of its radical repudiation of the Christian ethic in favor of a political-moral sensibility of violent retaliation and black nationhood. Baraka's is expressed more in terms of an African-derived religiosity that discomposes dogma and theology in favor of an ethos of total immediacy and expressiveness.

As the new black literary intellectuals of the 1960s traversed the road from «Negroness» to «Blackness,» they reenacted in contemporary terms a historical set of responses to their New World condition: anger and celebration. But the experience also involved a metamorphosis of the old pattern as black American anger merged with the Third World rage directed against the white West, and as the celebrative impulse attached itself to the Pan-African vision of a redemptive Negritude.

This is the dual «mythic» truth that emerges from the personal experiences and styles of Gayle's and Baraka's accounts and that may be found reenacted in so many autobiographical stories of the decade. Cutting across social and cultural lines as well as sex, it animates the narratives of the Southern bourgeois Leslie Alexander Lacy and the proletarian «prison graduates» of Northern and Western urban backgrounds no less than those of the new Afro-American women appearing on the scene in the late 1960s, especially Nikki Giovanni, Angela Davis, and Maya Angelou. Out of the «Negro-to-Black» conversion experience, black autobiographers helped fashion a seminal story archetype whose creative energy fueled Afro-American writing in all genres in that turbulent decade.

Notes

[1] William E. Cross, Jr., «The Negro-to-Black Conversion Experience,» *The Death of White Sociology,* ed. Joyce A. Ladner (New York: Random House, 1973), pp. 267-86. Originally published in *Black World,* July 1971.

[2] Addison Gayle, Jr., «The Son of My Father,» *The Black Situation* (New York: Horizon Press, 1970). LeRoi Jones/Amiri Baraka, «The Heretics,» *The System of Dante's Hell* (New York: Grove Press, 1963, 1965). Though related to the rest of the material in *The Black Situation* and *System,* both narratives are structurally self-contained and autonomous works.

[3] Ralph Ellison, *Invisible Man,* chap. 10 (the hospital scene). (Harmondsworth: Penguin, 1965.)

[4] Theodore R. Hudson, *From LeRoi Jones to Amiri Baraka: The Literary Works* (Durham, N.C.: Duke Univ. Press, 1973), p. 111.

[5] Kimberly W. Benston, *Baraka: The Renegade and the Mask* (New Haven and London: Yale Univ. Press, 1976), p. 30.

[6] Jerome Klinkowitz, *Literary Disruptions: The Making of a Post-Contemporary American Fiction* (Urbana: Univ. of Illinois Press, 1975), p. 105.

4

Toward the Post-Protest Novel:
The Fiction of John A. Williams

The student of Afro-American fiction after 1960 is fortunate in having the *oeuvre* of John A. Williams. With all due respect to the individuality of his talent, it would seem fair to say that his achievement offers, to a degree rarely seen, the paradigm of a decade. To so stress the typicality of the work and the career is not to imply a bowing agreement to the ideological and artistic orthodoxies of the age. Examples of independent stances and opposition to the dictates of Black Cultural Nationalism and the Black Arts Movement are not hard to come by. What lends to Williams's achievement its quality of representativeness is the central presence of the major issues and tensions of the period and the struggle one senses in the later works to create novelistic equivalents of racial, social, and political urgencies. After *Sissie* (1963), each new book reads increasingly as an effort to bend and stretch the fictional medium so as to accommodate his vision of an unprecedented historical situation and the painful choices it inflicts on sensitive black Americans. The challenge fueling the author's imaginative powers is the invention of narrative modes capable of expressing the sense of reality of blacks living simultaneously under hazardous conditions inside a white America willfully opposing historical change and in a larger world rapidly becoming post-Western and «afterwhite.» Affected by the simultaneous backlashes of neocolonialism abroad and racial repression at home, the emergence of Third World vistas, and the revival of revolutionary nationalist sentiments, the conditions of black authorship changed drastically in the course of the decade.

Williams's early work is conceived within the framework of traditional protest writing. Becoming more boldly experimental after *Sissie,* it may be seen to parallel in broad outline the general currents observable in American narrative art in this period. One recognizes in his stories, as the decade progresses, the same pull of nonrealistic modes that operated in novel writing generally. The

impulse to move narrative toward fantasy and fabulation is increasingly felt after 1965, although at no point did his formal experi-
mentation lead to the break with representationalism seen in the
radical avant-garde experiments with myth and parable, metafic-
tion, or parody. This fidelity to representational realism, originating perhaps in his long journalistic experience and interest in
history and politics, helps explain the attraction for Williams of
another major genre in the 60s: the nonfiction novel. Anticipated
by his use of Charlie Parker's life story for his early jazz novel
(*Night Song,* 1961), the documentary impulse grew increasingly
stronger with the mounting political pressures of the second half
of the decade.

It must be emphasized, however, that if Williams's work
reflects the rapid changing of rules that occurred in American
narrative art in this period, this must — if one wishes to preserve a
sense of the particularity of his achievement — be seen in terms of
its responses to the special pressures working on the black artist.
Such pressures throw light on the rather sharp cleavage which
occurs in his work between *Sissie* and *The Man Who Cried I Am*
(1967).

With the rise of Black Nationalism, changing geopolitical
perspectives, and a «post-Negro,» «Afro-American» consciousness, Williams's narratives underwent a metamorphosis, substitu-
ting for the protest formula new structures that frequently mixed
fantasy and documentary. As anger at injustice gave way to sus-
picions of a white conspiracy, the early fiction of moral outcry
yielded to new forms in *The Man Who Cried I Am* and *Sons of
Darkness, Sons of Light* (1969). Only by thus transforming the
novel of racial protest could the torrent of rage unleashed by the
consciousness of a pervasive and malevolent racism in the Western
world be accommodated. At the same time, celebration of the
black heritage could no longer be adequately expressed in fictional
evocations of the folk in the vein of Charles Chesnutt, Jean
Toomer, and Zora Neale Hurston. Responding to the urgent call
for a celebrative affirmation of black America in *Captain Blackman* (1972), Williams weaves a historical fable spanning two centuries of heroic black involvement in the nation's wars, as docu-
mented by transcripts of actual source materials and acted out in
the gigantically expanded mind of a single fictive and allegorical

soldier-hero present and participating in every major war since 1776.

Thus it is important to recognize that although Williams's work conforms in important respects to general mainstream currents, some of the thrusts towards documentary as well as nonrealistic modes of writing are of a different order. The spirit of his fabulations is not the darkly comic one of writers like Joseph Heller, John Barth, Thomas Pynchon, or Kurt Vonnegut. On the other hand, his nonfictional fiction must be distinguished both from Norman Mailer's compulsion in *The Armies of the Night* to turn the reporter into the hero of the tale and Truman Capote's aloof stance and cult of objective graphic description of visible surfaces in *In Cold Blood.* Intimately involved as his work was in the turbulent changes in Afro-America in the 1960s, the spirit informing the new departures in his craftsmanship after *Sissie* can only be properly gauged in terms of the special pressures on the black writer to be *engagé* to which it was submitted. In a manner typical of the decade, that engagement expressed itself in a profound and lucid wrath superseding the moral indignation of traditional protest art as well as in passionate eulogies of the race's survival strength and *soul* beauty.

The reformist anger informing Williams's early work — *The Angry Ones* (1960), *Night Song,* and *Sissie* — coincides rather closely with the prevailing mood of the civil rights era, and may be conveniently observed in his travelogue of 1963, *This Is My Country Too,* and in the 1962 edition of an anthology he compiled and prefaced for The New American Library, *The Angry Black.* His odyssey across America for *Holiday* magazine ends on a note of hope and guardedly optimistic commitment to a continued search for an America that «has as yet to sing its greatest song.» Similarly, in the preface to *The Angry Black,* his concern is to channel anger into fruitful uses by deducing from it its underlying causes. Properly interpreted, anger may lead to a truer understanding of black reality, «the morality of the situation will then resolve itself, and truth, which is what we all presumably are after, will then be served. This done we may all be able to rid ourselves of the illusion and delusion with which we've lived for so long a time.» The whole collection is viewed as «a probe beyond anger, a reaching for reason» which, it is hoped, will correct faulty per-

ception and promote action, so that the problem may be settled on
a rational and moral basis.

What Williams is affirming in these early statements is the validity for black writing of the protest tradition and its sociological
and moral premises. A climate of belief in integration, amelioristic
reform, and black-white alliances still dominated the Negro
intellectual community, encouraging a literature of social comment with implications of moral pleading. Against this background, Williams's choice of the framework of the protest novel
for his first creative efforts was a logical one.

The debt of Williams's apprentice fiction to the protest tradition
is particularly evident in its most distinctive structural peculiarity:
a persistent duality of characterization and plotting. Each of the
three novels features a character pair whose fates develop along
contrastive curves. After *Sissie,* this pattern disappears, and in
Sons of Darkness, Sons of Light (1969) and *Captain Blackman*
(1972) it is entirely absent.

Admitted by the author himself to be a conspicuous element,
this presence of a «tandem pair of black guys»[1] is explained as a
practical method to render a wider range of black speech as well as
providing him with a «confidant» for use in dramatic scenes and
in character presentation.

However, helpful though the author's comments are, the fuller
literary significance of this structural bipolarity emerges more
clearly when viewed in generic terms as related to the division that
has always existed within Negro protest writing between «uplift»
and naturalistic narratives. In the first, based on a moral vision of
society and human nature, character depiction and plot structure
stop short of complete determinism. Enough resilience remains in
the protagonist to make his story one of ultimate triumph over ad-
verse circumstances. The world is a testing ground for human
character, and aesthetic devices seek to record as faithfully as
possible the encounter of self and society.

The second strain of protest writing found its intellectual valida-
tion in the philosophical scepticism and scientific world view emerging in the late nineteenth century. The literary rendering of
human character is controlled by the concept of man as victim and
stated in terms drawn from abnormal psychology. Plots tend to
read like inventories of incidents of oppression and destructive

acts, frequently ending in destruction, anonymity, or sellout. Archetypally present in Booker T. Washington's *Up From Slavery* (1900) and Paul Laurence Dunbar's *The Sport of the Gods* (1902), the two-story patterns run through the whole subsequent history of Negro protest writing. This is the twin pattern reproduced with increasing skill in Williams's first three novels, providing th fledgling author with a supportive structural framework. A brief examination will bring this out more clearly.

In a loosely plotted slice-of-life narrative, *The Angry Ones* chronicles the parallel struggles of two black characters claiming their rights in the hostile white world of New York City. The simplest and most schematically worked out story line is that of Obie's downfall. From a precariously held position as a college-educated journalist and magazine editor, the protagonist topples downward into the gutter of the city and eventual suicide. His movements constitute an urban odyssey of rejection, unemployment, menial jobs, and degrading poverty, driving him inexorably into self-deprecation and paranoia.

In contrast to Obie's story, that of Steve Hill is projected as the moral struggle of a resourceful, but imperiled self, as suggested by his name. From his initial pitiful state as a jobless bum in Los Angeles, he rises through a succession of ordeals to a knowledge of the world and an understanding of himself. He emerges from the crucible of racial oppression a more deeply humanized being, capable of empathy and sharing and of perceiving his own struggle in the larger context of bettering conditions for future generations.

Night Song, published the following year, represents a substantial improvement over *The Angry Ones* both in terms of plotting and characterization. The story is told from the limited omniscient point of view of David Hillary, a white English professor whose academic fortunes have declined sharply as a result of heavy drinking. Living his derelict life in Greenwich Village, he finds himself drawn into the orbit of the lives of two black characters, the gifted jazz musician Richie Stokes, nicknamed Eagle, and his friend, a black bourgeois dropout named Keele Robinson.

Despite Williams's effort to make Hillary a Jamesian central intelligence whose initiation and moral education are of some importance in their own right, the novel's chief locus of interest is the bipolar story pattern involving the lives of the Charlie Parker-

based character of Eagle and his ultimately successful friend.
Eagle's story reaches a skillfully dramatized climax in chapter 14.
Disillusioned by Hillary's white liberal cowardice in failing to
stand up for him, he puts on a ludicrous act of self-parody, acting
out the «nigger» role in full view of the crowd at the Rockefeller
Plaza. The performance is designed to bring to light the invisible
scars of the black American victim: self-hatred, the confused mix-
ture of lucidity and paranoia, and the nihilistic loss of any sense of
order and trust. It should be noted, however, that Williams makes
a deliberate effort to make the character of Eagle transcend a
simple formula statement of the psychology of oppression of the
racial victim. Drawing on a characteristic contemporary trend observable in the work of Baldwin and Kelley, the author attempts to
elevate the black musician to the level of a shamanesque figure, investing him with a touch of redemptive madness whose power continues to operate in the lives of surviving characters after his
death.

Keele Robinson, an idealist disillusioned with bourgeois life and
organized religion, has dropped out of his respectable career. His
quest takes him into the Village underworld of jazz, junk, and human misery, where he finds himself involved in two conflicting
relationships with his jazz musician friend and a white mistress,
Della. Having internalized the negative self-concept thrust on him
by his environment, he vents his deep-seated rage on Della, «short-
circuits» his ability to function sexually with her, and retreats into
a self-made shell of indiscriminate antiwhite hatred and self-
hatred. From this nadir, he rises to the challenge of restoring his
self-confidence and trust in human goodwill.

Overcoming the temptation to blame everything on the oppressor, Keele struggles through to genuine self-understanding and to a
compassionate attitude toward Della and even Hillary. In an ending somewhat marred by sentimentality, Keele ends his self-
imposed exile by finding safe anchorage in the haven of married
love. Ultimately, however, Keele emerges with the contours of a
character tension-filled enough to indicate the author's beginning
liberation from formula and stereotype. Enough of Keele's troubles are of his own making, and his powers of self-analysis sufficient to make his development one of earned moral *ascesis,* in contrast to Eagle, against whom the forces conspiring are externalized

in the predatory record manufacturers, club owners, jazz critics, and white women forever hovering near him.

Initially, *Sissie* might appear to present a problem in that it does not feature an individual character pair in the same clear-cut manner. This difficulty is easily resolved, however, once it is realized that the pair in this novel is a generational one. The story places Sissie and Big Ralph Joplin alongside their children, Iris and Ralph, structuring the story of the parent generation within the conventions of naturalistic protest, whereas the lives of the young Joplins are cast in terms of a plot of moral tribulation and overcoming against heavy odds. Though marking a substantial advance over the first two novels in its more sophisticated handling of time sequences and irony as well as in its renunciation of sentimental and melodramatic effects, *Sissie* is dependent on the same narrative duality.

The parents' story is that of life under Mississippi's Jim Crow system, uprooting, and transplantation to the Northern city. Conceived within the traditional naturalistic mold of the oppressed pariah, the plot records the incidents of racial discrimination confining the Joplins to Bloodfield. This was the urban ghetto aptly named after the tract of land outside the city walls of Jerusalem purchased by the high priests with the money returned by Judas after his betrayal of Christ, a place inhabited by lepers and used as a burial ground for aliens. Big Ralph's story follows the familiar course of the progressive disintegration of the victim under oppression. The portrait of Sissie, however, finally transcends formula. Though ensnared in the same forces that condition her husband's life, she is involved in an experience too complex to make it one of mere survival. An innate impetuosity accounts for a significant portion of the suffering she undergoes as well as inflicts on her husband and children. Also, constitutionally incapable of fatalistic resignation, she refuses to see her life as a failure, not out of perverse pride, but because she has a fundamental respect for people and faith in the inherent nobility of even the damaged life. In his dexterous handling of the ending of Sissie's story, Williams takes creative liberties with the naturalistic plot. Though she is made to die, the manner of her death is not dictated by the demands of either philosophical determinism or racial polemic. Dramatizing the last encounter between mother and children in a muted and ambiguous deathbed scene, the author bends convention to the needs of life itself by weaving a varicolored tapestry of melancholy, homage to the black matriarch, and tangled emotions between the generations.

The lives of the young Joplins follow different courses before they are brought together at their mother's deathbed. Essentially, however, their stories move along parallel tracks designed to elicit the reader's sympathy for two black American artists struggling and overcoming. Pealing off layer after layer of time through the use of reminiscence and flashback as Iris and Ralph fly West (literally as well as symbolically), the novel maneuvers them into confrontation with the family and racial past, making them aware of the weight of that past as they try to find anchorage in a white world suppressing black artistic creativity. Faced with the effects of racism in family life, the armed forces, mental institutions, marriage, and the world of art (show business and the theatre), Williams's two artist-heroes are cast as agents in mutually reinforcing plots charting their moral progress and ultimate triumph.

Such, then, is the structural dichotomy controlling the author's early work. On the one hand, victim stories ending in annihilation (Obie), martyrdom (Eagle), or an ambiguous death (Sissie). On the other, moving along a parallel but ascending track, *Bildungs*-stories in which the recurring pattern is that of a black moral self doing battle with a hostile environment and emerging victorious, however tenuous the victory. For both plot types, Williams draws heavily on the world of art to supply locales as well as characters. Again and again, his protest against the actual or threatened waste of black American humanity is dramatized in stories of defeated or successfully struggling artist or artistlike heroes. The only exception is Sissie. In stories of the making or the breaking of the black artist, the young Williams found the most effective image of the high stakes in the struggle of his race for equal rights.

The superseding of the civil rights movement by a militant and separatist Black Nationalism, a white backlash at home and abroad, a succession of «hot summers,» and the emancipation of the Third World led to a profound intellectual and artistic crisis among New World blacks in the mid-sixties. In a potentially revolutionary domestic situation accompanied by the opening up of new geopolitical vistas, it was imperative to redefine the role of the Afro-American artist. Belletristic modes of writing as well as old-style protest found themselves irreparably discredited as the Black Arts movement arose, loudly proclaiming the need for a new racial art simultaneously combative and celebrative in form and spirit.

Although at no time commanding the loyalties of all black writers, the new ideas did contribute to a shared climate of artistic thought and expression in the second half of the decade. For Williams, too, this upheaval was a decisive influence. Intimations of this revolution of sensibility may be observed in his preface to the second edition of the 1962 anthology, symbolically retitled *Beyond the Angry Black* (1966), in which the language of reason and morality has been superseded by a vocabulary of apocalypse because, it was now felt, «sheer *anger* could never be enough to *right things. I pleaded* for *reason.* I feel that that *argument,* too, has failed. One cannot reason with those who have no use for reason» (italics added).

Williams's statement contains the key concepts of the rhetoric of protest discarded by so many black artists during the mid-1960s. To be oppressed and in the right had always provided the sociological and moral rationale for the two story patterns of victimized pariahs and ultimately triumphant black virtue in distress. With the bankruptcy of the art of moral outcry, the challenge to the black novelist's inventive powers was that of fashioning forms capable of accommodating a rage beyond mere righteous anger and a spirit of joyful celebration of the race's new-found *soul* beauty and cultural autonomy.

William's work in the second half of the decade revolves around these two sources of creative inspiration. Underlying and unifying all his postprotest work, however, one finds a distinctive tendency to fuse a documentary and reportorial style with an impetus toward fantasy. Whether the tone of the narrative is combative or celebrative, settings, events, and characters oscillate between exposé and fabulation. Instead of stories of sufferers and pleaders, the author invents new fictions combining accurately reconstructed actuality, futuristic scenarios, slow-moving realistic plots, fast-paced thriller action, and characters who may be either lifelike representations or abstract, allegorical figures.

The Man Who Cried I Am chronicles in panoramic fashion the collective story of black America since 1940 as it is filtered through the mind of a sensitive and intellectual hero, the journalist and novelist Max Reddick. His educational odyssey includes failed love affairs and professional successes as well as involvement in major national events from the Second World War to President Kennedy's administration and its aftermath. For Max the turning point is August 28, 1963, a day saturated with ominous interlocking public and private ironies. Within that day, whose official focus is the March on Washington, four other incidents occur that ironically convey the illusory nature of that liberal political event. Enzkwu, the African diplomat possessing knowledge of the Alliance Blanc and the American King Alfred Plan designed «to terminate, once and for all, the Minority threat to the whole of the American society, and indeed, the Free World,» is killed. In Nkruma's Ghana, Du Bois — the man who prophesied that «the problem of the Twentieth Century is the problem of the color-line» — dies. Margrit Westoever returns to Holland, her marriage to Max in shambles under the pressures of racism. And finally, on that day, Max is informed that his cancer tests are positive, that — symbolically — the infectious germ lodged in his body when he, as a young man, entered white America and accepted its premises, is malignant. At the end of the story, Max dies, fully conscious that his death at the hands of an America going fascist is appropriately symbolic of his former delusion that the proclaimed new frontiers and squarer deals were meant to include black Americans. The same malignant germ that has been operating in his body has also been operating in the body politic. With sure tragic instinct, the author handles Max's last hours. The moment of recognition comes too late to occasion a recovery. The disease is too far advanced. But at least he dies aware of the forces that have shaped his fate and of the error of judgement that has contributed to his downfall.

What such a bald paraphrase can only hope to suggest is the inexorable thrust, skillfully actualized in the narrative, of Max's development toward a total understanding demystifying the operations of white power in history an in the present. The author projects a protagonist who, for all his contemporary authenticity, is a deliberately created abstraction of heroic omniscience more characteristic of fantasy than of the semidocumentary realism that encapsulates the story. The ultimate nonrealism of Max Reddick as a fictional character conception is evident early in the story in the author's calculated omission of information concerning his hero's childhood and youth and in the equally deliberate absence of psychological interiority and intimacy. Such particularizing details are replaced by symbolic imagery making Max a hero of almost superhuman clairvoyance and rage.

The most obvious, though easily overlooked, symbolism is that of Max's profession. As conceived by Williams, his protagonist is less an agent involved in a fictional plot than a journalistic camera eye and purveyor of the «inside story» of the black race in the Western world. His accumulated reminiscences read like the truthful exposé of an era, recovered «as it really was,» the story of the observer-reporter «who was there.» He functions as a sort of reader's stand-in and the intermediary through whom are reported not just facts but truth as the reader witnesses the repercussions of historical events on Max's imagination. Williams's rhetorical strategy is that of involving us in the process of history becoming truth as it is lived through by the observer on the spot and supplied with the depth that his keen historical intelligence can contribute. Throughout, the authority of the portrait of Max Reddick derives more from the reader's confidence in his power to retrieve and interpret actuality than from his psychological or moral credibility. Williams casts his hero as a reportorial witness to the times , whose story is simultaneously expositional and corrective. The ultimate purpose of Max's recalled story is not just to recover the postwar era, but to show black America's illusory commitment to its liberal face and alert the racial community to future dangers.

The note of Max Reddick as a truthseer of heroic lucidity is sounded repeatedly. Technically, it is managed through a recurrent pattern of comments made by minor characters. «Look at old Max. Digging it all. . . . That's what you are Max, a noticer, a digger of scenes. Max the Digger,» Harry Ames says, and Zutkin, a New York Jewish intellectual, adds later: «He has a memory like a Jew . . . just as Jews remember back to Babylonia and Egypt and beyond, up to the present.» Such statements are counterpointed by Max's own self-descriptions, by his symbolic as well as literal marksmanship and hunting skill, and by Williams's tendency to present him in thoughtful, reflective postures. Finally, it is implied in Max's self-conscious identification with two seers of ultimate truth, Charlie Parker and, especially, Benito Cereno. A Yeatsian visionary watching the rough beast slouching toward Bethlehem to be born as he is being hunted down and shot by two black henchmen of the CIA, Max is shown in full possession of the ultimate secret of Western civilization with regard to black people: its readiness to resort to «final» and «genocidal» solutions. His knowledge is indeed that of Melville's hero, «saddened beyond death.»

The analogy with the Spanish sea captain is also illuminating in bringing out the nature of the rage that is Max Reddick's response to «this seeing precisely,» as he describes his lucid state before death. Just as his historical knowledge is preternatural, so his rage transcends personal grievances to become a «mythic» emotion. Seeing and knowing produce in Max an extraordinary heaviness of mind that goes beyond the merely moral and reformist anger of protest fiction victims. As Max confronts the accumulated histori- cal evidence of white racist destruction, his feeling grows to a ti- tanic and impersonal wrath at the thought of slain sons and ravished daughters over the centuries. Its innermost quality is curiously unaggressive, partaking rather of the nature of a deep and lingering sorrow. Strangely, Max Reddick emerges a kind of mourner, carrying the burden of a collective regret that a survival politics of violent retaliation should be forced upon black America. It is a state beyond hate («He knew he did not hate...») or moral indignation, a sadness or bottomless grief at the sight of the massive damage done to the race. Max's emotion belongs in a realm far beyond that of the Bigger Thomases of black protest. Laboring under the weight of personally felt injustice («Why should they have what we ain't got?»), they react in the only manner available to them — an instinctive hatred of the oppressor. The mournful rage of Williams's hero flows from a different source: his laser-beam insight into how, in June Jordan's 1969 words, «we were chosen, weighed and measured, pinched, bent backwards, under heel . . . (how) we were named: by forced dispersal of the seed, by burial of history, by crippling individuali- ty that led the rulers into crimes of dollar blood.»[2]

A mutilation of such magnitude Max can only see in genocidal terms. On one level, such an apocalyptic and conspiratorial vision may be regarded as part of a common and even fashionable mode both in fiction and film in the late 1960s and early 1970s. It must be admitted that the last part of *The Man Who Cried I Am* is not invulnerable to charges of surrendering to ephemeral popular moods. At the same time, however, one must bear in mind Williams's concern with the right of blacks to define their own past. Throughout the novel, Max is resentful of the white and Jewish «plot» to deny Afro-Americans the right to the concept of genocide by limiting it to the Six Million. To Max (and to the author, one feels), this is just another example of the historical plunder of the black race and its right to name its own condition.

However, Max's rage-filled knowledge extends beyond this to an understanding of black complicity in the damage and to his own personal implication in the corruption. This total consciousness of the black condition is expressed in a pattern of interlocking images of historical and private circles, strategically woven int the opening and closing scenes. Appropriately symbolic, the initial presentation of Max Reddick features him somberly reflecting in an Amsterdam restaurant three hundred years after the Dutch sold John Rolfe's fellow colonists «twenty negars» and three years after the dissolution of his marriage to one of their descendants. «Come full circle on the Dutch,» he ruefully observes while waiting for Maggie. Shortly afterwards, she appears in his dream lying with smoking filter-tipped cigarettes in her vagina on a conveyor belt that goes round and round, and from which he flees in a state of panic. Finally, he sees his terminal cancer of the rectum as a «vicious cycle,» aware of the symbolic implication of a diseased anality in his participation in the white man's world of success and liberal illusions.

In the final thrillerlike scene, Max is hunted down and shot by two black CIA agents, thus externalizing the idea of a guilty Negro complicity. The shoot-out closes the circle of his career, symbolically begun with another shooting match on the occasion in 1940, of his first admission to the glamorous world of literary success. Invited to a prestigious New York intellectual cocktail party, the young Max willingly acquiesced when urged to challenge Harry Ames, his black literary «father,» in a contest staged by the white audience. The incident dramatizes the syndrome of white manipulation and Negro acquiescence in the literary marketplace, symbolically counterpointed and extended in the intrablack show-down in the last chapter.

But Williams's thriller finale also reintroduces and reinforces Max's self-consciously circular perception in the opening scene. Clutching his gun and shooting for the balls of his fellow blacks, he sees the whole situation bitterly in terms of a closing-in move-ment, an «ultimate trap»: «This is the final irony. The coming of age. Negro set at Negro in the name of God and Country.» At this moment, Max is no longer merely a knower of the demystified truth of white racist power, the Negro's historical burial, and his own abetment. He has himself *become* the circle of that truth, bearing its scars on his own body.

The drama of dying that unfolds in the last pages of the novel transcends personal death. To speak in the idiom of the 1960s, it involves the demise of the masquerade identity of «Negroness,» externalized in the caricatured character of Professor Bazzam and heard as the voice of Samione (i.e., Sambo-in-one) in Max's stream-of-consciousness passages. Face to face with the gathering momentum of malevolent white power, he recalls Moses Boat-wright, a black Jean Genet-like intellectual, whose urgent call for a «Black» exodus from «Negro» illusions he failed to heed. The only legacy Max can bequeath is his rage-filled and mournful understanding, and the hope that it may survive to become the basis of postprotest «Black» action.

Sons of Darkness, Sons of Light continues the exploration of an increasingly insane racist reality, pursuing the theme of black rage further into the realm of politics while at the same time striking a new note of celebration of the moral and cultural resources of the race. The vision in search of literary form is one of malevolent white power actually erupting within a diseased social organism. The Indian and the Jew having outlived their usefulness as scape-goats, American civilization is depicted as reenacting a familiar historical drama, this time with the black cast in the role of public sacrificial villain. In a real sense, the story of Eugene Browning picks up where that of Max Reddick leaves off — with a sense of impending disaster. In *The Man Who Cried I Am,* Williams had sought in the concluding chapters to capture the experience of an imminent calamity in a world going mad by employing the conventions of the spy story, a genre specifically designed to convey a precatastrophic reality at the point where the disaster seems close. Much of the technical apparatus of the genre is easily identified: proximity to the world of diplomatic and political intrigue, intelligence networks and conspiracies, electronic surveillance, cinematic simultaneity of events and scenes, and a suspense-filled plot thriving on fast motion, violence, chase, and showdown.

The creative challenge in *Sons of Darkness, Sons of Light* is to forge a fiction in which the apocalyptic events can be shown as actually occurring and possible consequences analyzed. In the story of the «Negro-to-Black» conversion of Eugene Browning, the black bourgeois official of a civil rights organization, Williams's search is for a form that can express both the actualities of a revolutionary situation and its inherent potentialities. The framework most congenial to this concern he constructed from the conventions of thriller writing and anti-Wellsian dystopias.

The affinities of Williams's novel with the thriller are easily seen. An apocalyptic mood and a persistent Manichaeism envelop the narrative, as suggested by the title and the epigraph, both of which refer to the vision, mentioned in the Dead Sea Scrolls, of a cosmic cataclysm, «the War of the Sons of Light Against the Sons of Darkness.» Further similarities are the straining toward allegory and the element of secrecy and dissembling prevalent in most of the characters: Browning, the Don, Millard Jessup, Leonard Trotman, Morris Green, and Itzhak Hod. The plotting, too, draws on the thriller formula: an opening *in medias res,* brief dramatic scenes in rapid succession, simultaneity, violence, and situational suspense.

Throughout the novel, such thriller-style features operate in concert with devices derived from the antiutopian novel. This is particularly evident in the futuristic element, the use of extrapolation, and the didactic-prophetic purpose. In the thriller, the disaster exists as an immanent possibility to be averted by the hero's revelation of the conspiracy. In the dystopian story, on the other hand, the catastrophe has arrived, either in the form of a totally rearranged social reality or as actually erupting eschatological events. In keeping with the latter mode, Williams's novel presents a picture of the end of a world in a holocaust of racial and civil war, focusing on the conflagration itself and the weeks immediate-

ly preceding it. From an outwardly quiet state, ripe with revolutionary tension, the situation escalates through a chain of events
triggered by Browning's act of selective violence into a full-scale
disaster.

This event is projected through the device of time travel. The
story, published in 1969, is set in the 1970s. The author's intention
is to draw a picture of a future within immediate reach and growing directly out of the present. The apocalypse is no abstraction or
distant prospect, it materializes within a world whose language
and institutions are those of our own time. By thus shortening the
temporal perspective, Williams invests his futuristic projection
with the immediacy and impact of current reality.

The features in the contemporary situation that are extrapolated
into this catastrophic scenario are the totalitarian trends in white
America and the response of the black community. White society
is epitomized in the character and behaviour of the German-
American killer Herman Mahler in Alabama and the predomi-
nantly Irish police force in New York. The mentality and ideology
ruling America are of a fascist kind. In chapter 11 there is
symbolic confrontation between the mayor of New York and the
city's police commissioner that shows the breakdown of liberal
politics in the face of mounting violence. The line that separates
the Police Benevolent Association from an outright fascist organization is so thin as to be almost nonexistent. To Hod, the Zionist
terrorist hired to kill a cop, the situation is clearly genocidal and
analogous to that of the Third Reich. Browning himself describes
his white compatriots as «fascists» whose law-enforcement offi-
cials act like brownshirts when they beat up peaceful black demon-
strators. The nation's legislatures are seen as passing laws in preparation for final «exterminations,» and «telephone operators and
postmen and everyone else is a part of the Gestapo system.» White
America is a totalitarian power structure whose fascist nature is
becoming increasingly visible, a system in crisis prepared to resort
to «final solutions» to eliminate racial minorities. This fascist analogy is reinforced by another, seen by the Don, a Sicilian-born
underdog character, between America and «the last days of
Pompeii, the fall of Rome.» The novel's vision is the double one
of American society as a fascist empire, a colossus resting precariously on feet of clay. In partial contrast to *The Man Who*

Cried I Am, the fascist-imperial analogy as used here appears facile. While Max Reddick's genocidal and conspiratorial vision is at least made understandable in the light of his extensive and mature experience, the use of this concept in *Sons of Darkness, Sons of Light* is, I feel, unearned and hackneyed.

The other major extrapolations from the contemporary situation are drawn from the Afro-American community: the crisis of the civil rights movement and the rise of black militancy. The symbol of the former is Browning's organization, the Institute of Racial Justice. The diagnosis of its lethargy includes not just the cadres of the organization itself, but the black bourgeoisie and the intelligentsia that supports and funds it. Bill Barton, its director, uses it for self-protection and career advancement to the point that he even cooperates with the FBI in return for secret financial assistance. The fund-raising tour undertaken by Browning is designed as an odyssey of disillusionment through the world of the black business and professional élites, big-time entertainers, star athletes, and socialites. Like Scott Fitzgerald in chapter 4 of *The Great Gatsby,* Williams uses names satirically to expose their owners' pretensions as a class: Braithwaite II, Hudson, Washington Lincoln, Turner, Drake, Bascombe, Blanton — an impeccable Anglo-Saxon list with an added dash of French elegance. Williams deals an even harder blow when he has the Don lecture Browning on their moral and intellectual vacuity. It is the traditional deception of black intellectuals, he says, that because they have minds they think they have «no use for the tough stuff.» Browning's awakening to the truth about himself and his social class is a pivotal point in the novel. It is a class suffering not only from social plagiarism, but from a softness at the core, a bourgeoisie whose names, identity, and manners are pastiches on the white world, an élite without inner substance or pride.

As in *The Man Who Cried I Am,* the hero's «Negro-to-Black» conversion in Williams's dystopian thriller scenario develops from his knowledge of the demystified truth of a conspiratorial white racism and of the complicity of the black bourgeoisie. Like Max Reddick, Eugene Browning finds himself catapulted from a state of righteous anger into deeper feelings of rage and horror. True to its generic conventions, however, *Sons of Darkness, Sons of Light* concerns itself less with emotional states than with the problems forced on the hero in devising a militant politics of rage. Williams puts his radicalized protagonist through an education during which he is faced with the perennial problems of revolutionary history. For example, what looks like a simple substitution of one moral principle for another — the *lex talionis* for the ethic of the other cheek — turns out to involve unsuspected complexities. The simple, clean, and selective act of retaliation, thought of as a warning, is a miscalculation. Snowballing into a massacre, it fails to achieve its intended goal. Violence is no abstraction to be used for symbolic purposes, nor are its consequences rationally controllable and predictable.

Browning also faces the temptation of sentimental indulgence in imported notions of urban guerilla tactics. Such ideas are satirized in the portrait of Dr. Millard Jessup, the ultimate Romantic. A successful doctor, living in grand style in the Baldwin Hill section of Los Angeles, he is involved in the organizing of secret guerilla groups. Entirely without political judgement, he accepts John Birch money, thinks his revolution will triumph overnight, and that the middleclass will rally with the masses behind the guerilla-led uprising. Jessup is a naif, a creator of «shock waves» unconcerned with «the desolation of the murderous reaction.» Hearing on the radio that Jessup's snipers have started a killing spree in Los Angeles, Browning reflects on the likely outcome of such tactics: «Ah, Jessup trying to draw the cops out there into Watts, perhaps, and then the people would do just as the people are doing elsewhere. Round robin: killaniggerkillacrackerkillaniggerkillacracker.»

Having rejected the dangerous innocence of the Romantic revolutionary, the novel proceeds to consider the deeper issue that a politics of black rage will have to face in the fully realized dystopian situation. In a scene placed at the outbreak of the racial holocaust, Greene and Trotman have arrived at a fatal point. A leader of the black struggle, Greene, for reasons of safety feels compelled to lock up his friend and coworker during a decisive operation. This act lays bare the troublesome issue that all revolutionaries must face. It is the perennial problem of the many human imperfections in political events — mistrust, fears, and jealousies. Every radical vision contains — in the words of Trotman — the desire to «change the goddam pattern . . . just to make it a different bag

altogether, to break the continuum jof revolutionary history.»
That had been their vision, too, «to take the fork in the road from
the white cats.» «What we had, we've got no more,» Trotman
says, coming out of the closet. «We've got the same kind of
revolution everyone else has had, haven't we? Well, shit, it
figured.»

Faced with the consequences of the conflagration he has helped
spark, Williams's embattled hero realizes that the translation of
black rage into politics is no simple matter. Browning is shown
going through a development that, while not denying the validity
of his rage, increasingly stresses black pride and celebration of the
resources of the Afro-American community. He reverses his position on the efficacy of political assassination, though the legitimacy of violence per se is upheld. The possession of firearms and
their use in self-defense is an obvious and accepted principle in his
revised creed as the family gather in their Connecticut retreat. A
rehabilitated confidence in knowledge and education replaces
direct terrorist action. Outlining his future plans to Bill Barton, he
reaffirms his loyalty to his former profession. Clearly, however,
the teaching he envisages is not that of a traditional liberal arts
eduction, but a committed and revisionist pedagogy, aimed at
demystifying white power and inculcating black pride: «I'm going
to teach down this system.»

The reconciliation of male and female and the reconstituting of
the black family unit on a new basis would seem to be another
resource to which Browning's eyes are opened. In a finale somewhat flawed by sentimentality, a new bond of cooperation and
mutual respect is established between husband and wife that
should be seen against the historical background of damaged
relations between the sexes under conditions of oppression.
Williams also has his black protagonist pay homage to the new
black woman in the portrait of his oldest daughter, significantly
named Nora. And he is shown proudly listening to a «soul sta-
tion» on his radio; out of it pours «real jazz with the great instru-
mentalists from another time,» the authentic racial music from before the time when «Chuck» adulterated it.

The final point to be raised is that of Williams's ambivalent
handling of the issue of black-white coalitions, so controversial in
the late 1960s. Wary of an exclusive racialism, he projects his

themes of black rage and celebration in a larger interracial context. Through Browning's experiment with selective violence, the novel dramatizes the familiar topic of an alliance of oppressed minorities. In allegorical fashion, the author creates typed portraits of a Jew, an Italian-American, and an Afro-American. Equipped with an equally valid set of grievances, Hod, the Don, and Browning join hands in a cooperative venture to rid society of the racist Carrigan. However, the coalition is not permitted to function outside an underworld of gangsterism and Mafia-like operations. On the other hand, the three characters are depicted as attractive figures whose «crimes» go unrevealed and unpenalized. It is as though, respectfully dismissing this traditional league of underdogs, Williams replaces it with another by approvingly including Woody Chance, Nora's white boyfriend. Woody represents that white countercultural generation to whom Eldridge Cleaver also appeals so hopefully in *Soul on Ice*. In the last chapter, he is admitted to the restored black family unit in their self-defensive battle against the common enemy — the American Moloch created by the generation of Woody's affluent parents and from which he has defected. It is a historically new black-white alliance without any sacrifice of black humanity, untainted but also untested, the uncertainty of which is suggested by Woody's last name.

Published in 1972, *Captain Blackman* shows the author ready to respond unequivocally to the nationalist impulse to celebrate the heroic dimensions of the Afro-American story. The novel is nothing less than a quest for the grand style of a racial epic capable of expressing the indomitable will to survive during three centuries in the New World. For this purpose, old-style evocations of the folk could be of only limited use. What was called for was a modern narrative form that could accommodate broad historical vistas as well as express a sense of black spiritual and cultural power. To achieve this ambition, Williams put to use the resources of oral storytelling. Not only are scenes involving performing black raconteurs included in the narrative itself, but the whole story is projected in the form of a tall tale, which gives the author the freedom to draw on the whole range of black history.

Though animated by the author's documentary passion, the book transcends realism to become an epic and affirmative celebration of Afro-America in a form exploiting the fantastic element in oral storytelling.

The story exploits the idea of the tall tale in the form of a dream vision. Opening *in medias* res as Captain Blackman is wounded in Vietnam, the plot follows a pattern of descent into the Hell of the black experience in America's wars, beginning with Concord and Lexington. The formal continuity of this journey through history in the hallucinatory vision of the wounded Blackman is secured by the reincarnated presence of Blackman himself in every major war since 1775 and by the recurrence of names of other characters: Griot, Black Antoine, David Harrison, Woodcock, Belmont, Doctorow, and Mimosa all reappear as names of characters living in subsequent times and wars. In the first stages of Blackman's plunge from the present, he is conscious of temporal discrepancies. Moving among his fellow black soldiers at Concord with a 1968 perspective on 1775 and subsequent history, he appears an oddity to them and to himself. In later wars, however, he blends entirely with the times, becoming one with the racial experience as it is reenacted with each new war. Occasional returns to the present serve to point up the distressing monotony of the story of racial oppression as well as to mark the contrast with the «neo-Black» spirit of the nineteensixties. With Vietnam, two centuries of black loyalty and trust in the nation's pledges come to an end. The Blackman who returns from his historical odyssey at the close of his literal and symbolic coma develops to become an «earth-shaker» and a «prime-mover,» who, ultimately, determines the fate of his symbolically named antagonist and former superior, Major Ishmael Whitman.

In *Captain Blackman,* the author's penchant for realism survives in a surface resemblance to historical documentary and the war novel. His debt to the former mode is most obviously reflected in the use of such authentic source materials as Army memos, newspaper clippings, and records of Congressional hearings. More important, however is the revisionist impulse so central to the story, as noted by Addison Gayle.[3] Whether concerned to document the neglected accomplishments of blacks in the settling of the West, bring to light the names and achievements of black troops in America's wars, or reveal shocking massacres, the author seeks in the manner of the revisionist historian to debunk and correct official images.

The conventions of war fiction are most easily observed in the numerous descriptions of combat and strategy. Battle scenes abound, drawn in a style deriving from the graphic accuracy of similar scenes in Hemingway's war writings and in the novels of World War II by Norman Mailer and James Jones. Furthermore, like the stories of Henry Fleming, John Andrews, and Frederick Henry, that of Williams's soldier-hero is constructed on the initiation principle tracing the process of his maturing under the pressures of combat.

Such resemblances to realistic styles of writing must not be exaggerated, however. On closer inspection, it becomes clear, for example, that the revisionist motive derives less from a desire to reconstruct the past rationally and dispassionately than from an ideological commitment to wrestle the control of historical images from the white usurpers. Seizing control of one's past is a key to identity and liberation in the present. Although facts abound, their purpose is primarily that of serving the Black Nation in a world of global racial conflict by furnishing a basis for heroic celebration. Similarly, the use of the framework of war fiction is ultimately rhetorical. The author seems to exploit the capacity of the genre for symbolic expression by turning the military story into a paradigm of the historical experience of New World blacks. In the manner of Heller's use of a World War II Air Force base as a symbolic microcosm of American society, *Captain Blackman* adopts military symbols as appropriate expressions of the black American condition. The story of Afro-America is one of organized racist power, violence, and subjugation behind a facade of official legitimacy within a social organization that — with reference to racial minorities — is reminiscent of an armed camp. The arbitrary justice, the manipulation, and the brutalities meted out to black Americans over the centuries can find no more proper symbolic equivalents than the court-martials, the smoke-filled staff rooms, and the MP bullies of a corrupt military organization.

The thrust to celebrate Afro-America is most directly reflected, however, in the manner of telling the story. Like a griot, or tribal bard, the novel addresses its black American audience claiming the offices of guardian of the race's historical memory and weaver of tales for its education. With complete narrative licence, time sequences are condensed, expanded, or disrupted, characters allegorized, and the point of view kept fluid in order to convey the multiple voice of the people. Spinning his story from the materials of the racial experience, the artist gives it back to the race as a loving tribute.

The actors in this composite historical pageant speak with the manifold voices of Afro-America, past and present, North and South. Collectively they define the racial experience in the New World. African origins, suffering, and the wisdom of the folk speak to us in the words and features of the raconteurs, and through a wide range of figures coming out of the world of blackness: plantation Negroes and urban sophisticates, soldiers and civilians, men and women. Their numbers include hustlers and «cool cats,» «bad» and «evil» characters, tricksters and conners, white-haters and idealists, cynics and optimists. A most varied assortment, they add up to a racial group portrait, drawn in a spirit of proud self-assertion.

The story and its actors are held together in the gigantically expanded memory of the hallucinating Abraham Blackman, making him the allegorical center of the book. The allegory is suggested in a number of ways, most obviously in his first and second names. Furthermore, his outward appearance is such as to compel unanimous admiration and respect: huge frame, strength, and dark complexion. His two-hundred-year record is «unblemished,» and Belmont, a young black soldier, recognizes unique regenerative powers in him: «You could make it a whole new army, a *new* one, man.» A Southerner by birth who joined the racial exodus to the Northern cities, he has now established his operational base in Africa. Having known both military and civilian careers, proletarian as well as middle-class life-styles, he comprises the group's social and professional story. «Dreamer, doer, believer» of epic stature, the character of Abraham Blackman embodies the racial experience.

The same epic-allegorical quality characterizes the major relationships of his life over two centuries. The relationships connecting him with the extraracial world are those with Ishmael Whitman and Man in the Rain. The treatment of the former is satiric in the extreme. Identifying the white man's ancestor as Hagar's son, the novel assigns to the master race a subordinate place in the genealogical and theological scheme of the Patriarchal story. An expelled son of Abraham and «a wild ass among men» (Gen. 16:12), Ishmael is both bastard and cursed. The white world's arrogant pretensions of divine favor and election are thus comically punctured. To this mocking deflation is added the comic detail that Blackman acts as map reader for his superior. Whitman is a reader of neither maps nor minds. In fact, he is a reader of nothing. Wholly dependent on force, he collapses in the final showdown with Blackman when the nuclear attack system is discovered to be out of order. He no longer has anything to throw at his enemy. It is the story of the bear all over again.

The relationship with the American Indian is dramatized in the concluding scene of chapter 7, constructed around the encounter between Blackman and Man in the Rain. Set in the as yet unsettled Western wilderness, its thematic overtones are the «mythic» ones of guilt, time, and retribution. It is a meeting of historical victims, with the actors cast allegorically as representatives of the two races. A sense of fate hangs heavily over the scene as they exchange words of prophetic import on their respective histories. Chided by the Comanche about his participation in the white man's exterminations, Blackman weakly fights off a sense of guilt by appealing to history and its entrapment of people and races: «Time captures all of us, Man in the Rain, and we do what we must.» The Indian prophecies the end of his people, pointing out the irony that the black race will survive and multiply because it submits to white domination. But the price will be too high. The day will come when the loss of freedom and dignity will be too heavy a burden to bear, and history will repeat itself. The black man will fight. Conscience-stricken, Blackman thinks: «That day would surely come, and if it did . . . the Indian could have his land back.» The scene betrays Blackman's feelings of guilt and ambivalence, of betrayal and historical necessity face to face with the aboriginal nonwhite population whose fate most closely resembles the story of Afro-America.

Blackman's most important intraracial relationships are with the Afro-American griots of the story and with Mimosa. Through the racial raconteurs, he is put in touch with his origins and true heritage. His dream journey contains three scenes of communal oral storytelling. In Book I, old Griot, «clown, raconteur, black patriot, ancient mariner,» tells his black New Orleans audience in the Baleine Noire that the sad tale of «Strachan, Ware n Martin» in the War of 1812. At midpoint the scene of Richard Boston's performing «Shine» before an all-black audience during World War I, is interpolated, and toward the end Linkey is shown reciting «The Signifying Monkey» to another black audience in the Second World War. Merging with the listeners, Blackman is initiated into the resources of black folk wisdom through tales of African and the Caribbean diaspora and of black American strongmen and tricksters.

The setting of Griot's tale is an inn where the talk is of «the black underside of the world,» of «the black kingdom of Haiti, of York's journey with Lewis and Clark, of distant African ports and hot tropical islands far to the South.» Behind a facade of apparent improvisation, the old raconteur's gestures and speech are conscious and calculated in keeping with his public role of turning hurt into laughter. To make his audience laugh to keep from crying is the sad, but time-honored office of the black jester, and Griot is a master of his craft. Having produced cathartic merriment in the audience, his performance finishes with Blackman offering Griot a ceremonial «hot rum.» The second scene is set in an overseas army barrack during World War I. «Shine» is recited by Richard Boston, «the company's raconteur,» in a performance that celebrates «the sheer joy of life the black boys had.» The storyteller's role and status is recognized by the audience, and the Olympian laughter aroused by his skill effectively expresses their rejoicing in the collective strength of the race and their contempt for «Charley.» The last recital is by Linkey, another raconteur, and occurs at a military base in San Francisco during the Second World War. He performs nightly, but is so skilled that each time an almost religiously expectant silence awaits the jester's arrival. He has «a big basso profound voice, and he could recite with all the nuances; it was easy to laugh night after night.» In accordance with recognized custom, Linkey claims the raconteur's prerogative of indulging in prefatory bantering and good-natured quarrels with his audience over a fee. In return, he so designs his performance as to express vicariously their wishful thoughts of desertion from the white man's army. But the jester sometimes plays his own game with the audience. This time Linkey chooses a version of «The Signifying Monkey» in which the monkey is killed by the lion.

This version he «dedicates» to Scovall, a black soldier who expresses resigned disbelief in the trickster-act Linkey says he is planning to escape. Scovall symbolizes the general envy and humiliation the black men feel at the storyteller's defiance of whites and the mood of defeatism prevalent among them. The whole scene is a subtle play on the emotions of audience and performer. Linkey's role is the educational one of administering the necessary criticism of Scovall's resignation as well as dramatizing a spirit of resistance. Under the circumstances, resistance must take the form of conning and wily ruse. Implicitly, the scene validates and celebrates the trickstertradition and its resources, rooted in the black folk culture and shown as fully capable of adaptation to modern conditions. Together the three scenes initiate the dreamer into the resources of the racial heritage extending back to slavery times and, through old Griot — a sort of racial ancestor figure — to the shores of Africa.

Only after this initiation has been achieved is the situation ripe for a restoration of healthy relations between the sexes within the racial group. After centuries of disrupted relations, Blackman and Mimosa of the 1960s eventually cement the black male-female union. The story takes care to distinguish the pristinely pure sex between these two archetypal representatives of the race from the degraded erotica occurring elsewhere. Mimosa's floral name appropriately suggests her earth-goddess-like naturalness, closing to corrupt sex and opening up to the fructifying touch of black virility. Their guiltless encounters are primeval events, the spasms of their orgasms a cosmic rhythm, and the phallus, «hard as a million-year-old stone,» an irrepressible power. Though vulnerable to charges of male chauvinism, the event of their union is described as an occasion of momentous importance, a measure of repaired damage and a new moral and social strength within the racial community, appropriately accompanied by Blackman's sense of having found his way home.

Emerging from his dream in which he has journeyed into the depths of the racial experience, he applies to the contemporary world the folk wisdom into which he has been initiated. That world, no less than the past, is one in which the cats and gorillas, rabbits and bears, monkeys and lions of black folklore confront each other in lethal conflicts. As realized by Max Reddick and

Eugene Browning in *Sons of Darkness, Sons of Light*, the price of
seeking admission to the world of the lion is high, almost fatal:
Blackman has lost a leg and damaged a lung. But his procreative
powers remain unharmed, and the folk experience provides a
guide to turning misjudgement and error into victory. His mode of
operation in the white jungle must be that of the «cool cat,»
speaking the enemy's language and piloting his planes while secret-
ly building the invisible Black Nation.

The final scene of the novel, entitled «The Tattoo,» dramatizes
the trickster-avenger stance adopted by Williams's hero. The scene
is a fantastic futuristic projection set in a world taken over by
blacks through the agency of light-skinned «passers» who have
infiltrated the white power system after training in Africa. Whitman's cumbersome technological society finds itself subverted
from the inside by the powerful and wily Blackman, assisted by
Woodcock. Characteristic ridicule is heaped on the white «bear»
in the description of Whitman's powerless fury, his deputy's
whimperings as he discovers that the nuclear attack system has
been dismantled («We've got nothing to throw at anybody, . . .
what posture should we take? We gotta have a posture»), and the
President's absurd preoccupation with being addressed in proper
English and his ultimate incomprehension («Listen to the silence.
It's almost like a noise. It's that goddam invisible busyness gone
from those secret things.») Behind the scenes, from his Third
World hiding place, Blackman issues the orders, and Woodcock,
nicknamed «Newblack,» implements them while singing huskily
«Way down upon de' Swanee Ripper.» It is a hilarious scenario
bringing into play the whole arsenal of ruse and put-on drawn
from the black folk tradition.

Ultimately, the novel is a paean to black soul power as a
humanistic and regenerative force in the insane world of the white
supremacists. A duplicate of Whitman's power would not be
worth celebrating. Blackman undertakes «to make it a different
road altogether, to break the continuum of revolutionary history,
to take the fork in the road from the white cats.» The ultimate
purpose is not to take over the enemy's murderous war machine,
but to dismantle it and offer to the world Afro-America's gift of a
new postwhite and post-Western humanism.

Captain Blackman brings to an end Williams's artistic journey in the 1960s, fusing the divergent and yet convergent impulses of the decade toward rage and celebration. Performing the office of literary «machine gunner»[4] in the war over historical images, the author simultaneously exults in the race's heroic will to survive. In the dream odyssey through time and space in Blackman's magnified memory and imagination, the story transcends its historicity to become a racial epic, the heightened tale of a people and its trials.

Notes

[1] Earl A. Cash, «The Evolution of a Black Writer: John A. Williams,» (Ph.D. dissertation, University of New Mexico, 1972), p. 193.

[2] June Jordan, *Civil Wars* (Boston: Beacon Press, 1981), p. 47.

[3] Addison Gayle, Jr., *The Way of the New World. The Black Novel in America* (Garden City, N.Y.: Doubleday, 1976), pp. 336-37.

[4] Gayle's term in *The Way of the New World.*

Selected Bibliography

Abrahams, Roger D. *Positively Black*. Englewood Cliffs,
N.J.: Prentice-Hall, 1970.
Angelou, Maya. *I Know Why the Caged Bird Sings*. New York:
Bantam Books, 1969.
Baldwin, James. *Another Country*. London: Corgi Books, 1965.
——— *Blues for Mister Charlie*. London: Corgi Books, 1966.
——— *The Fire Next Time*. New York: Dell, 1964.
——— *Go Tell It on the Mountain*. London: Corgi Books, 1963.
——— *Going to Meet the Man* New York: Dell, 1966.
——— *Nobody Knows My Name*. New York: Dell, 1963.
——— *Notes of a Native Son*. New York: Bantam Books, 1964.
Baker, Houston A., Jr. *Singers of Daybreak. Studies in Black
American Literature*. Washington, D.C.: Howard University Press, 1974.
Baraka, Imamu Amiri. *See* Jones, LeRoi.
Baxandall, Lee, ed. *Radical Perspectives in Art*. Harmondsworth:
Pelican, 1972.
Benston, Kimberly W. *The Renegade and the Mask*. New Haven
and London: Yale University Press, 1976.
Berghahn, Marion. *Images of Africa in Black American Literature*.
London: *The Macmillan Co., 1977.*
Bone, Robert A. *The Negro Novel in America*. New Haven and
London: Yale University Press, 1965.
Bontemps, Arna. «The New Black Renaissance.» *Negro Digest,* 13
(1961): 52-58.
Brown, Claude. *Manchild in the Promised Land*. New York: The New
American Library, 1965.
Butterfield, Stephen. *Black Autobiography in America*. Amherst:
University of Massachusetts Press, 1974.
Chapman, Abraham, ed. *Black Voices*. New York: The New American
Library, 1968.
——— *New Black Voices*. New York: The New American Library, 1972.
Chesnutt, Charles. *The Conjure Woman*. Ann Arbor: University
of Michigan Press, 1969.
Clarke, John Henrik. «The New Afro-American Nationalism».
Freedomways 1(1961): 285-95.
Cook, Mercer, and Henderson, Stephen E. *The Black Militant
Writer in Africa and the United States*. Madison:
University of Wisconsin Press, 1969.

Cooke, M.G., ed. *Modern Black Novelists.* Englewood Cliffs,
      N.J.: Prentice-Hall, 1971.
Cleaver, Eldridge *Soul on Ice.* New York: Dell, 1968.
Cruse, Harold. *The Crisis of the Negro Intellectual.* New York:
      William Morrow & Co., 1967.
——— *Rebellion or Revolution.* New York: William Morrow & Co., 1968.
Davis, Arthur P. *From the Dark Tower. Afro-American Writers
      1900 to 1960.* Washington, D.C.: Howard University Press, 1974.
——— «Integration and Race Literature». *Phylon,* 17 (1956): 141-46.
Douglass, Frederick. *Narrative of the Life of Frederick Douglass,
      an American Slave.* New York: The New American Library, 1968.
Dunbar, Paul Laurence. *The Sport of the Gods.* New York:
      Collier Books, 1970.
Elkins, Stanley. *Slavery. A Problem in American Institutional
      and Intellectual Life.* New York: Grosset & Dunlap, 1963.
Ellison, Ralph. *Invisible Man.* Harmondsworth: Penguin, 1965.
——— *Shadow and Act.* New York: The New American Library, 1964.
Fanon, Frantz. *Black Skin White Masks.* London: Paladin, 1970.
——— *The Wretched of the Earth.* Harmondsworth: Penguin, 1967.
Frazier, E. Franklin. *Black Bourgeoisie.* New York: The Free Press, 1957.
Gayle, Addison, Jr.
——— *The Black Situation.* New York: Horizon Press, 1970.
——— *The Way of the New World. The Black
      Novel in America* Garden City, N.Y.: Anchor Press/Doubleday, 1976.
——— *Wayward Child. A Personal Odyssey.*
      Garden City, N.Y.: Anchor Press/Doubleday, 1977.
Gayle, Addison, Jr., ed. *The Black Aesthetic.* Garden City, N.Y.:
      Doubleday & Co., 1972.
——— *Black Expression.* New York: Weybright & Talley, 1969.
Gibson, Donald B., ed. *Five Black Writers. Essays on Wright,
      Ellison, Baldwin, Hughes, and LeRoi Jones.* New York:
      New York University Press, 1970.
Giovanni, Nikki. *Gemini.* New York: The Viking Press, 1971.
Great Slave Narratives. Selected and introduced by Arna
      Bontemps. Boston: Beacon Press, 1969.
Gross, Seymour L., and Hardy, John Edward, eds. *Images of the
      Negro in American Literature.* Chicago and London: University
      of Chicago Press, 1966.
Hansberry, Lorraine. *A Raisin in the Sun.* New York: The New
      American Library, 1959.
Hemenway, Robert, ed. *The Black Novelist.* Columbus, Ohio:
      Charles E. Merrill Publishing Co., 1970.
Hill, Herbert, ed. *Black Voices.* London: Elek Books, 1964.

Hudson, Theodore R. *From LeRoi Jones to Amiri Baraka: The Literary Works*. Durham N.C.: Duke University Press, 1973.

Huggins, Nathan Irvin. *Harlem Renaissance*. London, Oxford, New York: Oxford University Press, 1971.

Isaacs, Harold R. *The New World of Negro Americans*. New York: The Viking Press, 1963.

Jahn, Janheinz. *Neo-African Literature. A History of Black Writing*. New York: Grove Press, 1968.

Jones, LeRoi. *The Baptism* and *The Toilet*. New York: William Morrow & Co., 1964.

––––– *Blues People*. New York: William Morrow & Co., 1963.

––––– *Dutchman* and *The Slave*. New York: William Morrow & Co., 1964.

––––– *Home: Social Essays*. New York: William Morrow & Co., 1966.

––––– *Raise Race Rays Raze*. New York: Vintage Books, 1972.

––––– *The System of Dante's Hell*. New York: Grove Press, 1966.

Jones, LeRoi and Neal, Larry, eds. *Black Fire. An Anthology of Afro-American Writing*. New York: William Morrow & Co., 1968.

Kelley, William Melvin. *Dancers on the Shore*. Chatham, N.J.: The Chatham Booksellers, 1964.

––––– *dem*. New York: Collier Books, 1969.

––––– *A Different Drummer*. Garden City, N.Y.: Doubleday & Co., 1969.

––––– *A Drop of Patience*. Chatham, N. J.: The Chatham Booksellers, 1965.

Kent, George. *Blackness and the Adventure of Western Culture*. Chicago: Third World Press, 1972.

Killens, John Oliver. *Black Man's Burden*. New York: Pocket Books, 1969.

King, Woodie, ed. *Black Short Story Anthology*. New York: The New American Library, 1972.

Klein, Marcus. *After Alienation. American Novels in Mid-Century*. Cleveland and New York: Meridian Books, 1962.

Klinkowitz, Jerome. *Literary Disruptions: The Making of a Post-Contemporary American Fiction*. Urbana: University of Illinois Press, 1975.

Lacy, Leslie Alexander. *The Rise and Fall of a Proper Negro*. New York: Pocket Books, 1971.

Ladner, Joyce A., ed. *The Death of White Sociology*. New York: Random House, 1973.

Major, Clarence, ed. *The New Black Poetry*. New York: International Publishers, 1969.

Malcolm X. *The Autobiography of Malcolm X*. New York: Grove Press, 1965.

Margolies, Edward. *Native Sons. A Critical Study of Twentieth-Century Negro American Authors*. Philadelphia and New York: J.B. Lippincott Co., 1968.

Moody, Anne. *Coming of Age in Mississippi.* New York: Dell, 1968.

Redmond, Eugene B. *Drumvoices: The Mission of Afro-American Poetry.* Garden City, N.Y.: Anchor Press/Doubleday, 1976.

Reed, Ishmael. *Flight to Canada.* New York: Random House, 1976.

——— *The Free-Lance Pallbearers.* New York: Doubleday & Co., 1967.

——— *Mumbo Jumbo.* New York: Avon Books, 1972.

Sanchez, Sonia, ed. *We Be Word Sorcerers.* New York: Bantam Books, 1973.

Smith, Sidonie. *Where I'm Bound. Patterns of Slavery and Freedom in Black American Autobiography.* Westport, Conn.: Greenwood Press, 1974.

Stampp, Kenneth. *The Peculiar Institution.* New York: Random House, 1956.

Three Negro Classics (Up From Slavery, The Souls of Black Folk, The Autobiography of an Ex-Colored Man). Introduced by John Hope Franklin. New York: Avon Books, 1965.

Toomer, Jean. *Cane.* New York: Harper & Row, 1969.

Williams, John A. *The Angry Ones.* New York: Pocket Books, 1970.

——— *Beyond the Angry Black.* New York: The New American Library, 1966.

——— *Captain Blackman.* Garden City, N.Y.: Doubleday & Co., 1972.

——— *Flashbacks.* New York: Anchor Press/Doubleday, 1974.

——— *The Man Who Cried I Am.* New York: The New American Library, 1967.

——— *Night Song.* London: Fontana Books, 1961.

——— *Sissie.* Garden City, N.Y.: Doubleday & Co., 1969.

——— *Sons of Darkness, Sons of Light.* New York: Pocket Books, 1970.

——— *This Is My Country Too.* New York: The New American Library, 1965.

Williams, Shirley Anne. *Give Birth to Brightness.* New York: Dial Press, 1972.

Wright, Richard. *Black Boy.* New York: The New American Library, 1951.

——— *Native Son.* New York: The New American Library, 1964.

——— *White Man Listen!* Garden City, N.Y.: Doubleday & Co., 1964.